First World War
and Army of Occupation
War Diary
France, Belgium and Germany

2 CAVALRY DIVISION
Divisional Troops
Royal Army Service Corps
2 Cavalry Division Auxiliary Horse Transport (575 Company A.S.C.)
9 June 1915 - 23 June 1919

WO95/1128/2

The Naval & Military Press Ltd
www.nmarchive.com
Published in association with The National Archives

Published by

The Naval & Military Press Ltd

Unit 10 Ridgewood Industrial Park,

Uckfield, East Sussex,

TN22 5QE England

Tel: +44 (0) 1825 749494

www.naval-military-press.com

www.nmarchive.com

This diary has been reprinted in facsimile from the original. Any imperfections are inevitably reproduced and the quality may fall short of modern type and cartographic standards.

© Crown Copyright
Images reproduced by permission of The National Archives, London, England, 2015.

Contents

Document type	Place/Title	Date From	Date To
Heading	WO95/1128/2		
Heading	2nd C.A.V. Div Troops No. 2. Cav Div. Aux Horse TPT Coy. 1915 Sep 1919 June (575 Coy ASC)		
Heading	2nd Cavalry Division Gun September 25-9-15 September 30-9-17		
Miscellaneous	Historical Records Army Sucice Corps in Accordance With A.D.S.T-S.T.181 Dt 15.10.16		
Miscellaneous	October 28.10.16 to 31st October 1916 We remained as a Company Loaded Somme Up With Ammt. as Bonnay.		
Miscellaneous	Appendix		
Miscellaneous	The attached memo From The Director of Transport is forwarded for Information.	23/07/1917	23/07/1917
Miscellaneous	A.D.S. & T Cavalry Corps	27/07/1917	27/07/1917
War Diary	Abbeville	25/09/1915	26/09/1915
War Diary	Aire Roquetoire	27/09/1915	27/09/1915
War Diary	Roquetoire	28/09/1915	19/10/1915
War Diary	Bout-de-La Ville	20/10/1915	20/12/1915
War Diary	Renescure	21/12/1915	28/12/1915
War Diary	Esquerdes	29/12/1915	29/12/1915
War Diary	Cuhem	30/12/1915	31/12/1915
War Diary	Val De Lumbres	01/06/1916	07/06/1916
War Diary	S Marie Cappel	08/06/1916	08/06/1916
War Diary	Reninghelst	09/06/1915	20/06/1915
War Diary	Val De Lumbres	20/06/1916	26/06/1916
Heading	War Diary of 2nd Cavalry Division Auxiliary Horse Transport Coy. From 1st July To 31st July. 1916. (Volume XXIII).		
War Diary	Hazebrouck	01/07/1916	31/07/1916
Heading	War Diary of 2nd Cav. Div. Aux, H.T. Coy. for August, 1916		
War Diary	Hazebrouck	01/08/1916	31/08/1916
Heading	War Diary of Auxiliary Horse Transport Company, A.S.C. 2nd Cavalry Division For September, 1916		
War Diary	Hazebrouck	01/09/1916	06/09/1916
War Diary	Hazebrouck For Allouagne	07/09/1916	07/09/1916
War Diary	Allouagne for Hernicourt	08/09/1916	08/09/1916
War Diary	Hernicourt for Aubermetz	09/09/1916	09/09/1916
War Diary	Aubermetz for Abbeville	10/09/1916	10/09/1916
War Diary	Abbeville for Picquigny	11/09/1916	11/09/1916
War Diary	Picquigny For Bonnay	12/09/1916	12/09/1916
War Diary	Bonnay	13/09/1916	30/09/1916
Heading	War Diary of 2nd Cavalry Aux. Horse Transport Coy. October 1916		
War Diary	Bonnay	01/10/1916	31/10/1916
Heading	War Diary of 2nd Cavalry Auxiliary Horse Transport Company. November, 1916. Vol 5		
War Diary	Bonnay	01/11/1916	07/11/1916
War Diary	Ville Sur Corbie	08/11/1916	08/11/1916
War Diary	Bussy	09/11/1916	09/11/1916

War Diary	Belloy	10/11/1916	10/11/1916
War Diary	Buigny St Maclon	11/11/1916	11/11/1916
War Diary	Voisin	12/11/1916	30/11/1916
Heading	War Diary of 2nd Cavalry Auxiliary Horse Transport Company. December 1916. Vol 6		
War Diary	Voisin	01/12/1916	05/12/1916
War Diary	Voisin & Dompierre	06/12/1916	31/12/1916
Heading	War Diary of 2nd Cavalry Auxiliary Horse Transport Company. January 1917 Vol. XXIX		
War Diary	Dompierre	01/01/1917	04/01/1917
War Diary	Dompierre & Voisin	05/01/1917	25/01/1917
War Diary	Dompierre	26/01/1917	31/01/1917
Heading	War Diary of 2nd Cavalry Auxiliary Horse Transport Coy. February, 1917 Vol. XXX.		
War Diary	Dompierre	01/02/1917	28/02/1917
Heading	War Diary of 2nd Cavalry Auxiliary Horse Transport Coy. March, 1917 Vol. XXXI.		
War Diary	Dompierre & Voisin	01/03/1917	07/03/1917
Heading	Dompierre	08/03/1917	31/03/1917
Heading	War Diary of 2nd Cavalry Auxiliary Horse Transport Company. April, 1917 Vol. XXXII.		
War Diary	Dompierre	01/04/1917	04/04/1917
War Diary	Dompierre	05/04/1917	06/04/1917
War Diary	G Wavans	07/04/1917	07/04/1917
War Diary	Wavans to Hem.	08/04/1917	08/04/1917
War Diary	Hem.	09/04/1917	09/04/1917
War Diary	Hem. & Grouches	10/04/1917	10/04/1917
War Diary	Grouches & Barly	11/04/1917	11/04/1917
War Diary	Barly & Grouches	12/04/1917	12/04/1917
War Diary	Grouches	13/04/1917	30/04/1917
Heading	War Diary of 2nd Cavalry Division Auxiliary Horse Transport Co., A.S.C. May, 1917-Vol. XXXIII.		
War Diary	Grouches	01/05/1917	11/05/1917
War Diary	Naours	12/05/1917	12/05/1917
War Diary	Aubigny	13/05/1917	13/05/1917
War Diary	La Motte	14/05/1917	14/05/1917
War Diary	Roisel	15/05/1917	31/05/1917
Heading	War Diary of 2nd Cav. Div. Aux. H.T. Coy. A S C. From 1st June To 30th June 1917 (Volume XXXIV)		
War Diary	Roisel	01/06/1917	30/06/1917
Heading	War Diary of 2nd Cavalry Divisional Auxiliary Horse Transport Coy A.S.C. From 1st July 1917 To 31st July 1917 (Volume XXXV).		
War Diary	Roisel	01/07/1917	08/07/1917
War Diary	Buire	09/07/1917	12/07/1917
War Diary	Suzanne	13/07/1917	13/07/1917
War Diary	Morlancourt	14/07/1917	14/07/1917
War Diary	Thievres	15/07/1917	15/07/1917
War Diary	Magnicourt-Sur-Canche	16/07/1917	29/07/1917
War Diary	Etree Wamin	30/07/1917	31/07/1917
Heading	War Diary of 2nd Cav Div. Auxiliary Horse Transport Coy A.S.C From 1 August 1917 To 31 August 1917 Volume XXXVI.		
War Diary	Etree Wamin	01/08/1917	31/08/1917
Heading	War Diary of 2nd Cav. Div. Aux. H.T. Coy A S C From 01/09/17 To 30/09/17 Volume XXXVII.		

War Diary	Etree Wamin	01/09/1917	11/09/1917
War Diary	Etree Wamin E. Monchel	12/09/1917	12/09/1917
War Diary	Monchel	13/09/1917	30/09/1917
Heading	War Diary of 2nd Cav. Div. Auxiliary Horse Transport Coy A.S.C. From 1st October To 31st October 1917 (Volume No 38)		
War Diary	Monchel	01/10/1917	07/10/1917
War Diary	Monchel To Ramicourt	08/10/1917	08/10/1917
War Diary	Ramicourt	09/10/1917	19/10/1917
War Diary	Ramicourt To Fm Leroy	20/10/1917	20/10/1917
War Diary	Fm Leory To St Leger	20/10/1917	20/10/1917
War Diary	St Leger To Buyon	21/09/1917	21/09/1917
War Diary	Buyon	22/10/1917	31/10/1917
War Diary	War Diary of 2nd Cav. Div. Auxiliary Horse Transport Coy. A.S.C. From 1st November 1917 To 30th November 1917 Volume No 39		
War Diary	Buyon	01/11/1917	16/11/1917
War Diary	Proyart	17/11/1917	17/11/1917
War Diary	Tertry	18/11/1917	20/11/1917
War Diary	Montecourt	21/11/1917	27/11/1917
War Diary	Boucly Near Tincourt	28/11/1917	30/11/1917
Heading	War Diary of 2nd Cav. Div Aux. H.T Coy A.S.C From 1st December 1918 To 31st December 1918 Volume No 40		
War Diary	Boucly Tincourt	01/12/1918	06/12/1918
War Diary	Cartigny	07/12/1918	07/12/1918
War Diary	Daours	08/12/1918	08/12/1918
War Diary	Buyon	09/12/1918	10/12/1918
War Diary	Saleux	11/12/1918	12/12/1918
War Diary	Vers.	13/12/1918	31/12/1918
Heading	War Diary of 2nd Cavalry Divisional Auxiliary Horse Transport Coy. From 1st January 1918 To 31st January 1918 Volume XLI		
War Diary	Vers	01/01/1918	05/01/1918
War Diary	Proyart	06/01/1918	08/01/1918
War Diary	Vers	09/01/1918	31/01/1918
Heading	War Diary of 2nd Cav Div. Aux H T Coy A S C From Feb. 1 To Feb 28 1918 Volume XXXXII		
War Diary	Vers	01/02/1918	02/02/1918
War Diary	For Proyart	03/02/1918	03/02/1918
War Diary	Proyart For Mons	04/02/1918	04/02/1918
War Diary	Mons	05/02/1918	09/02/1918
War Diary	Mons en Chaussee	10/02/1918	24/02/1918
War Diary	War Diary 2nd Cavalry Divisional Auxiliary Horse Transport Coy From March 1st 1918 To March 31st 1918 Volume To XXXXIII		
War Diary	Mons en Chaussee	01/03/1918	13/03/1918
War Diary	Maucourt	14/03/1918	24/03/1918
War Diary	Maucourt For Bailly	25/03/1918	25/03/1918
War Diary	Compiegne	26/03/1918	27/03/1918
War Diary	Jonquieres	28/03/1918	29/03/1918
War Diary	Nuvers St Martin	30/03/1918	30/03/1918
War Diary	Plachy Buyon	31/03/1918	31/03/1918
Heading	War Diary of 2nd Cavalry Divisional Auxiliary Horse Transport Coy From April 1st 1918 To April 30th 1918 Volume To XLIV		

War Diary	Plachy	01/04/1918	02/04/1918
War Diary	Rivery	03/04/1918	05/04/1918
War Diary	Ailly Le Haut Clochier	06/04/1918	06/04/1918
War Diary	Eaucourt	11/04/1918	12/04/1918
War Diary	Valux	13/04/1918	16/04/1918
War Diary	Le Ponchel	17/04/1918	24/04/1918
War Diary	Vitz Villeroy	25/04/1918	29/04/1918
War Diary	Crepy	30/04/1918	30/04/1918
Heading	War Diary of 2nd Cavalry Divisional Auxiliary Horse Transport Coy A S C From 1 May 1918 To 31st May 1918 Volume No XLV		
War Diary	Enguinegatte	01/05/1918	04/05/1918
War Diary	Montcavrel	05/05/1918	31/05/1918
Heading	War Diary of 2nd Cavalry Divisional Auxiliary Horse Transport Coy From June 1st 1918 To June 30th 1918 Volume To XLVI		
War Diary	Montcavrel	01/06/1918	30/06/1918
Heading	War Diary of 2nd Cavalry Divisional Auxiliary Horse Transport Coy A.S.C From 1st July 1918 To 31 July 1918 Volume XLVII.		
War Diary	Montcavrel	01/07/1918	11/07/1918
War Diary	Brexent	12/07/1918	14/07/1918
War Diary	Wail	15/07/1918	15/07/1918
War Diary	Berlencourt	16/07/1918	22/07/1918
War Diary	Wail	23/07/1918	23/07/1918
War Diary	Alette	24/07/1918	31/07/1918
Heading	War Diary of 2nd Cavalry Divisional Auxiliary Horse Transport Coy From August 1st 1918 To August 31 1918 Volume No. XLVIII		
War Diary	Alette	01/08/1918	04/08/1918
War Diary	Repechy	05/08/1918	05/08/1918
War Diary	Caours	06/08/1918	06/08/1918
War Diary	Buigny	07/08/1918	08/08/1918
War Diary	Montieres	09/08/1918	15/08/1918
War Diary	Belloy	16/08/1918	16/08/1918
War Diary	Canaples	17/08/1918	17/08/1918
War Diary	Caumont	18/08/1918	22/08/1918
War Diary	Grenas To Bailleumont	23/08/1918	23/08/1918
War Diary	Bailleumont	24/08/1918	25/08/1918
War Diary	Grenas	26/08/1918	31/08/1918
War Diary	War Diary of 2nd Cavalry Divisional Auxiliary Horse Transport Company From 1st September 1918 To 30th September 1918 Volumn No XLIX		
War Diary	Grenas	01/09/1918	30/09/1918
Heading	War Diary of 2nd Cavalry Divisional Auxiliary Horse Transport Coy From 1 October 1918 To 31st October 1918 Volume No. L		
War Diary	Grenas	01/10/1918	18/10/1918
War Diary	Pas	19/10/1918	31/10/1918
Heading	War Diary of 2nd Cavalry Divisional Auxiliary Horse Transport Coy A S C From 1 November1st 1918 to November 30 1918 Volume No LI		
War Diary	Pas	01/11/1918	06/11/1918
War Diary	Bihucourt to Cambrai	07/11/1918	08/11/1918
War Diary	Bousies	13/11/1918	14/11/1918
War Diary	Tasmeres	15/11/1918	15/11/1918

War Diary	Douzies	16/11/1918	16/11/1918
War Diary	Maubeuge	17/11/1918	17/11/1918
War Diary	Thuin	18/11/1918	18/11/1918
War Diary	Morialme	19/11/1918	27/11/1918
War Diary	Waha	28/11/1918	30/11/1918
Heading	War Diary of 2nd Cavalry Divisional Aux H.T. Coy From 1st December To 31 December Volume No. LII		
War Diary	Waha	01/12/1918	15/12/1918
War Diary	Vieuxville	16/12/1918	16/12/1918
War Diary	Mont	17/12/1918	31/12/1918
Heading	War Diary of 2nd Cavalry Divisional Auxiliary Horse Transport Coy From 1st January 1919 To 31st January 1919 Volume (LIII)		
War Diary	Mont	01/01/1919	31/01/1919
Heading	War Diary of 2nd Cavalry Divisional Auxiliary Horse Transport Company From 1st February 1919 To 28th February 1919 (Volume LIV).		
War Diary	Mont	01/02/1919	28/02/1919
Heading	War Diary of 2nd Cavalry Divisional Auxiliary Horse Transport Company From 1st March 1919 To 31st March 1919 (Volume LV)		
War Diary	Mont	01/03/1919	06/03/1919
War Diary	Goffontaine	07/03/1919	31/03/1919
Heading	War Diary of 2nd Cavalry Divisional Auxiliary Horse Transport Company From 1st April 1919 To 30th April 1919 Volume (LVII)		
War Diary	Goffontaine	01/04/1919	15/04/1919
War Diary	Pepinster	16/04/1919	30/04/1919
War Diary	Pepinster (Belgium)	01/05/1919	31/05/1919
War Diary	Billets Pepinster	01/06/1919	23/06/1919

WD 95/1128/2

2ND CAV. DIV Troops
___

NO. 2. CAV DIV.
AUX HORSE TPT COY.
1915 SEP ~~1916 JULY~~ -1919 ~~APRIL~~ JUNE

(575 COY ASC)

(NO BOY)

MISSING 1916 JAN TO MAY

Cav 2.575 COV 3 France 4.

HISTORICAL RECORDS

Aux. H. T. Coy. A.S.C.
2d Cavalry Divisional

from ~~September 25.9.15~~
~~October 26.10.16~~

to September 30. 17.

Sheet.
1. Oct + November. 16
2 + 3. November. 16
4 December. 16
5 January 17
6.7 + 8 February 17
9. March 17
10.11.12.13 + 14 April 17
15 + 16 May 17
17 June 17
18 July 17
19. 20 + 21. August 17.

Historical Record. Army Service Corps.
In accordance with A.D.S.T - S.T. 181
of 15.10.16.

Unit 2nd Cavalry Divisional. Aux. H. T. Co A.S.C.

Para 1931 K.R.
(1) The company was formed at ABBEVILLE on 25th September 1915.
It was intended to use the company for the purpose of carrying Horse blankets for the Units of Cavalry, R.H.A. and Divisional Troops in the Division and 3 wagons were set apart to carry G.S. Blankets for the
(three) 3 Brigade Field Ambulance sections
Two of the companies were formed about the same time, 3 for the English Cavalry Divisions and 2 for the Indian Cavalry Division.
These Companies were only
to be used for carrying blankets during the winter months and were to be broken up in the Spring.

(11) The Company was recruited from the A.H.T Depot at ABBEVILLE, The Warrant Officer and a few of the N.C.Os. were regulars, the remainder were recruits, half of whom were practically untrained and knew nothing about A.S.C. Drivers work. The majority of these Drivers had arrived in France

(ii) Continued.

during July and August 1915.
The Depot at ABBEVILLE was so short of A.S.C. men at the time, that the establishment could not be made up and 18 men were attached from the Cavalry Regiment to make up the numbers. This number was subsequently increased to 34 Cavalry men.

(iii) The company left ABBEVILLE at 2 P.M on the 26th September 1915, the day after it was formed, having entrained in the morning and arrived, after being partly derailed at LA-PUGNOY, at its destination AIRE at 11-30 P.M on the 26th, the derailed portion of the train arriving at 6 A.M. 27th inst.

After detraining the company marched into camp at ROQUETOIRE.

The following are the stations at which it has been employed with dates of arrival and departure.

ROQUETOIRE	from 27-9-15	to	19-10-15
BOUT-DE-LA-VILLE	" 19-10-15	"	20-12-15
RENESCURE	" 20-12-15	"	27-12-15
ESQUERDES	" 27-12-15	"	29-12-15
CUHEM	" 29-12-15	"	4-1-16
CENSE-LA-VALLE	" 4-1-16	"	16-2-16
CLOQUANT	" 16-2-16	"	21-5-16
VAL-DE-LUMBRES	" 21-5-16	"	22-6-16
St MARIE CAPPEL	" 27-6-16		

BETHUNE

3.

(III) continued

YPRES

RENINGHELST from 8-6-16 to 19-6-16
VAL-DE-LUMBRES " 19-6-16 . 28-6-16
HAZEBROUCK " 28-6-16 . 4-9-16
ABBEVILLE via ALLOUAGNE - HERRICOURT -
HUBERMETZ   4-9-16 . 10-9-16
ABBEVILLE to BONNAY via PICQUIGNY
                10-9-16 to 12-9-16

SOMME

Still at BONNAY on despatch of this report.

(IV) The 2nd Cav. Div. Aux H.T. Coy A.S.C has accompanied the 2nd Cavalry Division since it first joined it at BOUT-DE-LA-VILLE - 19-10-15.

It has taken part in the following operations:

1. Attached to the Dismounted Cavalry Division, operating from SAILLY-LA-BOURSE. BETHUNE-AREA - 1st Corps from 7-1-16 to 16-3-16.

2. The Company H.Q and a few wagons were attached to the 2nd Dismounted Cavalry Brigade during its operations to the EAST of RENINGHELST in conjunction with the 3rd Canadian Division from 8-6-16 to 19-6-16.

3. On arrival of the company at BONNAY - SOMME-AREA. IV Army on 12-9-16 it was ~~formed~~ turned into an Ammunition Column and the wagons

IV continued.
were loaded up with 13 P.R. Shell & Bombs and Small Arm Ammunition.

V VI VII VIII No remarks.

IX 1. A draft or rather reinforcements to the number of 54 A.S.C. drivers arrived on the 23-6-16 to replace the 54 Cavalrymen, who had been doing A.S.C. work almost since the company was first formed.

2. On 26-6-16 an additional section consisting of 4 G.S. wagons with Tanks water mounted on them arrived from A.H.T. Depot ABBEVILLE. These were drawn by Mules and had R.F.A drivers - 15 drivers and 30 mules. This arrangement it was stated was only temporary during the summer while the company was being used as a water carrying company. Tanks & wagons were all handed over to O.C. A.H.T. Depot ABBEVILLE on 10-9-16. and a fresh issue made by him of 40 wagons G.S without Tanks.

The additional sect. of 4 wagons was also included in this and remained with the company, making a total of 44 G.S. wagons.

At the moment of writing these are loaded up with ammunition.

5

(X) This company is a mule company and it is understood the only mule company of the 5 formed.

The work of the company from shortly after its formation until about the end of June 1916 consisted chiefly in assisting the regimental transport of the various units in the Division in drawing rations, forage, wood and coal and in many instances in doing their fatigue work.

The OC found it exceedingly unsatisfactory for him from a point of discipline and efficiency to have nearly his whole company split up all over the Divisional Area and his men and animals at the beck and call of almost any N.C.O in any unit. The drivers were frequently called upon and made to do duties which they were not intended to do and in more instances than one severely punished for hesitating to do so. Wagons were constantly broken almost to pieces carting gravel and materials for building Squadron Stables and no attempt was made to repair them and when they could be no longer be used at all requisitions for new wagons were sent in to the Q.M. of this company.

In addition to this wagons were employed to cart wood and coal to Divisional Dumps and a

(x) continued.

good many were employed on
R.E. duties bringing up material
for the trenches.

At the end of July 1916 it
had been decided that this company
was to be made into a water tank
company and all wagons which
were out on duty were returned
and rejoined Coy H.Q at HAZEBROUCK
on the 28 - 29 & 30 July 1916.

Water tanks were issued, these
were of the round type and made
of corrugated iron. They were of
200 Gall capacity and several
different ~~types~~ shapes and quite unsuitable
for mounting on G.S. wagons. The
O.C. 2nd Field Squadron RE sent
a party to help in fitting these tanks
and after a fortnights united effort
we managed to get the tanks fixed
firmly on the wagons.

On filling the tanks with water
with the pumps which were also fixed
on the wagons, it was found that
they nearly all leaked badly and
that some would not hold water at all.

Solder was then applied for
and several tin smiths obtained &
O.C. 2nd Army Workshops also assisted,
in a fortnight all the joints were
re-soldered and even then it was
found that the tanks would not
hold water and they leaked at the

(X) continued
joints and especially underneath.
Reports were being constantly sent in and as a result it was decided to cast this issue of Tanks, called No 1 Patt: and they were handed in to O.C. R.E Park at STRAZEELE in the beginning of August.

Shortly after a new issue of tanks was made called M⁰ 2 pattern about 30-7-16. These were oblong in shape very much stronger than M⁰ 1, and much more suitable for fixing on wagons.

Unfortunately they had two holes for the taps bored in the broadest side of the Tanks and taps could not be fitted to them as this necessitated new holes being punched in the back or narrow side of all the 40 Tanks and the old holes plugged up again.

The O/c 2ⁿᵈ Army Heavy Workshops assisted in doing these alterations and fitted the taps but it was a long and difficult job and was only completed on the 25ᵗʰ August. 1916

By the end of the month all the tanks had again been properly fixed and the company was reported as being ready to move.

On the 5ᵗʰ September orders were received from H.Q 2ⁿᵈ Cav: Div to be ready to march to ST VENANT this was cancelled on evening of 6ᵗʰ

8/

and orders were given to remove all tanks from the wagons at once and hand them in at STRAZEELE Siding. On the 7th this order was carried out and half the tanks were removed and all the fittings of the other loosened. At about 10-30 AM an urgent order was received to replace tanks on wagons immediately and be ready to proceed by route march via AILOUAGNE & HERNICOURT O.C. to ABBEVILLE and hand the tanks and wagons complete over to the O.C. A.H.T Depot on 10-9-16. This was done and 40 G S wagons were issued in their place.

The company marched out of ABBEVILLE the following morning with orders to proceed to BONNAY (Somme Area) via PICQUIGNY.

Arrived at BONNAY on evening of 12-9-16 and found the Divⁿ there.

On the following morning orders were received that the company had been converted into an Auxiliary Ammunition Column and that the following ammunition must be drawn and loaded at once.

  13 Pr. H.E 1350
    " Shrapnel 1350.
  Bombs N° 5 1800.
  S.A.A. 534,000 rnds.

This was loaded up on 36 wagons. We were also to carry 2 wagon loads

a.

continued.
of spare parts for guns but this was subsequently cancelled.

We then became a reserve ammunition column to the R.H.A. ammunition columns for the push. The company remained at BONNAY from this time and was still parked there on the 30-10-16 when this was written

Lieut. J.R. Govett the only other officer in the company proceeds to England on transfer to Royal Artillery after serving with the company since its formation and takes with him the best wishes of the O.C. and all ranks of the 2nd Cav. Div. Aux. H.T.

It is considered that the heavy loads of ammunition at present loaded on the wagons is far too big a load for 4 mules some of which are scarcely 13 Hands high. Teams of 6 mules are required, the same as all other ammunition columns have.

October
26.10.16. to 31st October 1916

SOMME

We remained as a Company loaded up with Ammn: at BONNAY.

NOVEMBER 1916

Still at Bonnay Camp. Somme.
On 1st November. Lieut F. PEPPER ASC arrived reports for duty with the Company & replace Lt Gorette. & takes over his duties.

Up to the 6th inst the Company or part of it is exercised daily in marching order. In spite of the very wet weather the mules are looking well & full of work.

On this day I have all the Ammn: overhauled & re-packed & the wagons cleaned out.

Orders are also received to rejoin the Division at VILLE SUR CORBIE on the following day.

The Company leaves BONNAY for good at 8 am on the following day by march route & proceeds to VIVIER MILL Railhead and then hands over all the Shell & Ammunition. This duty was completed by 12 noon under the direction of Lt Pepper & S.S.M. Hickie. ASC. The Company then proceeded to VILLE SUR CORBIE & re-joined the Division there & camped bivouacked up to our knees in mud in the pouring rain. During the afternoon, of the same day. 8 teams were issued to each of the 3 Brigades & 4 to the R.H.A Bde. to assist them in carrying kits & Baggage to the Back Area – 2 others to OC. ASC & 2 to Div. H.Q.

2

NOVEMBER

3 Teams were left behind with the Dismounted Cavalry Park, and 4 Teams with the 20th Divl. Artillery.

On the following day (8th inst) the remainder of the Company viz 8 Wagons paraded at 10.30 am & marched in rear of the Division. Through CORBIE & camped in the fields in the vicinity of BUSSY for the night. Very cold & wet.

On Thursday 9th inst we marched to BELLOY via AMIENS - AILLY - St SAUVOEUR & LA CHAUSSÉE.

On Friday 10th inst we marched from BELLOY to ABBEY due North of ABBEVILLE. ~~& marched for the night~~ where we found our bivouacks occupied we eventually camped at BUIGNY St MACLOU.

On Saturday, 11th inst we had a fine day for a change and proceeded on our long days march to VOISIN which is really part of DOMPIERRE arriving about 1 pm. It was a pleasant days march through the CRECY FOREST & reminded us of the times of the Black Prince as we passed the Mound where he is supposed to have stood to watch the battle in 1679 (?)

At DOMPIERRE we take up our winter quarters which are very bad indeed taking them all round.

3

NOVEMBER.

We are all glad however to get under almost any kind of shelter as most of us had lived in the open for over 2 months & the weather had been exceptionally cold & wet nearly all the time. The mules & horses of this Company had stuck this bad weather + too much wet + were probably the fittest of any in the Division. We had been lucky during the part of the 2 months we spent at Bonnay when the weather was so bad, in being able to get to make good standings either in farm yards or on bits of unused roads, wherever possible, sheltered from the wind. The result was that the mules kept their condition & it was possible to get to them & groom them & the men had not to stand over their boots in mud as was the case in many other units & corps.

The next day (12th inst) our wagons & 7 mules & big men returned by rail from dismounted Cavalry Party, and during the week more of the teams returned from the units. On 18 inst the Div Comdr. Major Gen. W. K. Bundy, inspected billets & expressed his satisfaction with all he saw. On 20th inst the Company commenced to draw wood & coal from various parts of the Country & this continued all through the winter. From 20 to 30 teams are employed almost daily for distances of from 10 to 24 miles.

4
December 1916

The beginning of December still finds the company hard at work at DOMPIERRE. Cutting wood & coal from CRECY forest & other woods and Coal chiefly from HESDIN, both these places are 10 miles away. As a rule it was drawn one day and distributed another to Troops &c —

Whenever possible efforts were made to improve mens billets also but the mens billets were pretty bad Stables & standings &. Clipping was also proceeded with vigorously, but as there was only one machine for 200 animals the progress was slow & it was decided only to clip them high to start with.

Xmas day & New Years day were no unusual but quiet events of the month & so 1916 ended —

5

January 1917

We commence the New Year of 1917 at our old billets at DOMPIERRE. The first half of January is cold but with now again a heavy snow storm. About the middle of the month hard frosts begin and on the 24th skating commenced on the ponds all round this continued for almost 6 weeks without a break.

The Company is employed all through January in carting Wood & Coal frequently for great distances that is to say over 20 miles a day & in some cases as much as 28 miles. Several days a week Wood has to be drawn out of the forests & is frequently most difficult to get to this weapons & teams get badly knocked about.

~~In addition to this work we are called upon to assist the M.T. & like wood cutting & forage work than when the BARIERT EERME is put into M.T. not allowed to be used. In spite of all this work~~

— The forage ration is reduced from 12 of hay & 12 of Oats to 9 lbs of Oats & 10 lbs of Hay. The exceeding cold weather combined with the excessive work & shortage of forage, begins to have a bad effect on the draught animals.

During this month 9 teams are still our attached to units chiefly 3rd Bde.

War Estabt of this Company is increased by 3 artificers & 6 drivers vide. W.O. letter of 6-1-17.

6
February 1917

The Company is still in the same billets as DOMPIERRE. The weather is extremely cold hard frost day & night up to 16th of February when a thaw & rain follows. This continues to the end of this month but the weather is cold.

The duties the company has to perform are practically the same as in January only more so. On account of thaw about 16th the Barriers are closed on the roads and the M.T. is to a great extent unable to deliver rations & forage to units.

A part of this extra haulage falls on the Divn. H.T. and this duty lasts off & on for a fortnight or three weeks, so as to give time to repair the roads and get the frost out of them. Some of the roads broke up very badly indeed the worst places were usually where there was a hill on the road. The Chalk which in this part of France seems to be the bed on which the metalling is laid is crumbled to powder when the thaw sets in & water oozes out of the road like milk & great holes are left which have to be filled up with metal.

No heavy vehicles of any kind are permitted on the roads during this period.

The "frost scheme" is brought into operation.

Boxing —

2
February 1917

Continued -

On 23rd inst at 3 p.m. I am informed that the A.D. of S&T will inspect the Company on 24th inst at 4 p.m. So we do not get much time. All ranks as usual work hard and well, with the result that the A.D. of S&T (Col Any croft) was thoroughly satisfied with what he saw & congratulated the company on the turn out & the condition of the Animals. Under the circumstances this was most satisfactory. It was a bitterly cold February day, the mules had been doing extremely hard work ever since November almost every day & the forage ration was only 9 lbs of oats & 10 lbs of which 2 lbs was local forage usually hay, when it was to be had at the price.

My personal opinion was that just about this time the mules had had about enough & there were several which were very much thinner than I cared to see them. About a week later this was very much more marked and a good many more fell off. I was beginning to feel very anxious about them and applied to O.C. S&C for extra corn which they were badly in need of & should certainly be given when doing extra hard Transport work in the winter.

animals
From what I saw and heard my Company compared most favourably with those of any other unit about this time.

8 February 1917 Continued.

There was a good deal going on in the boxing line and several of the drivers got left in for the Divl Show the principals were being Tatlock & Burke both did very well the latter knocked out 4 or 5 men in almost as many minutes. They were both aft in for the Divl Competition. Here Burke had bad luck & I think should have won but Tatlock did better and was deputed to represent the Divn in the light weights at the Cav Corps Show. at Abbeville, which was most creditable.

We also had a fairly good football team but not the best pluck.

Sgt Major to write.

9
March 1917

There was a heavy fall of snow on 5th March but it soon melted away. About we had frost & snow again on 7th inst and this lasted for several days. About 11th the weather became much milder and some really fine days, but after that frost & mixed weather continued until the end of the month.

So far as the Company work was concerned there was just about the same amount of the same kind as we had in Jan & Feby. Carting Coal & wood &c and distributing it to the various Brigade Dumps & units.

March was a very flat & uninteresting month but we were cheered up about on 17th when the news arrived of the Capture of BAPAUME by the British.

Gas drills & inspection of Gas appliances caused some excitement, but perhaps the 3 days boxing at ABBEVILLE for the Cov. Corps Championship caused the greatest interest as the Company representative D. Tattock ran into the semi final & was only beaten by the man who won at that weight.

On the 14th inst I received a great shock on being informed that on again moving into the Forward Area the company would have to carry the following in future. 825 sacks of Oats (@ 80 lbs) & 620 boxes of Iron Rations (@ 70 lbs). These were drawn from HESDIN on 18th & 19th inst. This was stored

10
April 1917

April was the ARRAS Gap
Scheme month, and the weather was
about as bad as it well could be
take it all round. There were about
five days to begin with but then the
rain started & turned into heavy snow
storms the worst of all being on the
afternoon & night of 11-12 inst - when it
lay for a foot thick over everything.
This snow formation continued, with high winds until the
24 or 25th with when the rain gradually
decreased & the end of the month was dry
& cold & windy -

On 3rd instructions were received
that the Company would carry ammunition
again for the "Gap scheme", and that the
825 Sacks f oats + 620 cases of iron
rations were to be handed over to a
Mobile Supply Column which was being
formed (viz 301.P.S. wagons) from units in
the Div - this is done.

On 4th inst Ammunition is drawn
from the Ammunition Column at WADICOURT
& loaded up & the balance delivered on the
following day. 2700 rounds of 13 pdr and
532,000 of S.A.A., also 2 wagon loads of
Spare parts for Guns - Orders to march
are cancelled but we finally did get
our fair Winter Quarters on 7th inst &
heavy DOMPIERRE at 11 am we went into
bivouacks at BEAUVOIR - RIVIERE near
WAVANS.

11 April 1917.

Continued.

Battle of ARRAS &c.

The Division moved on the Easter Sunday next day & we followed him (at 3pm) on ~~Sunday (first)~~ with instructions to bivouac at OCCOCHES which we reached after many delays about 6 p.m. in rear of the whole of B. Echelon. This place was crowded with troops & much further delay was caused by wagons remaining on the main Road in ~~rest~~ while billets were being detailed following it.

The Town Major of this place did not evidently expect so many troops and ~~then~~ informed me that no more accommodation was available. He advised me to go on to a place called HEM where we arrived at 7.30 p.m. and made ourselves fairly comfortable. On this day the Company came under the orders of Cav. Corps, & daily wires, as to ammunition in stock, have to be sent in by 12 noon.

The Company remained at HEM until Tuesday afternoon (10th inst.) when sudden orders arrived to march at once to GROUCHES. We arrive at GROUCHES in rear of B. Echelon at 5pm. There is a great scramble for billets but eventually get under cover. Roads are very bad here & no proper place can be found to park the wagons. Cold & wet day. On Wednesday about 12 noon the D.A.A.Q.M.G. arrives on a visit & is surprised to find that I had not received orders to move before. He instructs me to move at once to BARLY near FOSSEUX. We start at 2.30 pm but have some delay in getting ~~the wagons out of this narrow bad lanes~~ loaded ammunition.

(Major Winkler arrived)

12
April 1917.

Continued.

As we leave GROUCHES a heavy snow storm is raging by far the worst of this year & one of the worst I have ever experienced. The snow was nearly a foot deep on the roads & continued to fall all the afternoon & evening. The storm was driving in our faces all the way and it was bitterly cold. S.S.M. Hickie & Q.M.S. Harper were sent on ahead and had made good arrangements for our accommodation when the Company arrived in BARLY at about 8 p.m. It was quite dark & we were again made to park the wagons in a very narrow lane with high banks & full of mud in spite of my protestations.

There was a good though very inconvenient stable which took most of the mules & the men were billeted in a barn further down the village. This was a very good afternoon & evening's work & the Drivers did their work most cheerfully & well under these very trying circumstances. The mules swung along in grand style in spite of their 6 hour load and the bad & heavy state of the roads. The distance travelled I estimated at 17 miles.

At midnight (11th - 12th) further orders arrived for the Company to return to GROUCHES as soon as possible.

On 12th marched back to GROUCHES by the same route as yesterday, where we arrived at 1. p.m. having covered 34 miles in 23 hours with heavily loaded wagons in bad roads

13
April 1917.

Continued

in the worst weather experienced during the war. This would have been done in much shorter time only for the difficulty of getting the Company out of the congested traffic in BARLY, the loading up of extra supplies & extra iron rations &c.

On 13th remained at GROUCHES. Had an inspection of animals & found them all in good condition with the exception of No 1 Sect which had not yet recovered from the hard work it had done in the winter while attached to 3rd Bde. Mules were bivouacked in a field but the men & horses were under cover.

On 16th the 5th Machine Gun Coy arrived in GROUCHES. On the same day instructions were received from Corps Cav to hand in 116,000 rounds S.A.A. & 1800 hand grenades. O.C. Ammn Coly took them over and his men unloaded & deposited them on a Corps Corps Dump. This reduced the loads by about 7½ Tons or some 5 Boxes a wagon.

Instructions were also received to hand over the Horse rugs to the Cavalry who were by this time in Stables. This was an inconvenience & particular hardship as the weather was still extremely cold & wet. The mules were clipped & standing without any protection in the open.

Horse rugs sent to R.S. Supply at LUCHEUX.
On 19th O.C. A.S.C. (Col. Scott-Elliot) arrived & inspected my mules. He also gave me instructions

14/
April 1917

Continued

to dump the Ammunition in a convenient place in GROUCHES and be ready to help in drawing supplies. The Supply Columns having been very much over-worked owing to many lorries out of action.

On 20th Ammunition is off loaded & 10 Teams are sent out to help 3rd Bde. on 21st inst. The 5th M.G. Sqn find a guard over the Ammunt.

The following are sent out during the next few days. 3 Teams to the Group at LUCHEUX. 2 Teams to 5th M.G. Sqn at GROUCHES. 10 Teams to PAS with 4th Cav. Bde. 3 Teams to M. Lanciers at WAVANS. We draw our supplies from rail-head at BOUQUEMAISON.

The Company remains at GROUCHES to the end of the month. The R.S. Guep [?] find men a guard for the Ammunt. on 30.

15
May 1917

H.Q.f

On 1st May the Company is still at GROUCHES where it remains until the 10th inst., on this day orders are received to make Brigades up to 12 Teams each + 4 To O.C. A.S.C. for various duties. This leaves 5 Teams with Coy. H.Q.

There are sents outs on 11th inst. + on 12th with the Divn. march to ROISEL — which is about 6 miles from ST QUINTIN via NAOURS — AUBIGNY + LAMOTTE —

The march was enjoyable and interesting & the weather was fine — The last day from LAMOTTE to ROISEL was particularly interesting as it was for the greater part through recently captured territory. The damage the Germans had done to roads &c. + villages was quite wanton + unnecessary from a military point of view. The rails had all been removed from the railway permanent ways + Telegraph posts cut down.

Can be elaborated on to any extent.

The distance covered this day 15th inst by the Divn. was roughly 25 miles. We arrived at ROISEL at 6 p.m. — Bivouacked in a field near the station —

The next day Teams were returned from Btns. + units. On 17th we commenced to keep the Divn. supplied from Rail Head — assisted by from 21 to 31 Limber Teams from 2nd Cav. Bde. R.P. — This work continued without change until the end of May —

King of Belgium

Continued

16
May 1917

The Minitos our cooking fuel well in spite of the weather which was not too good. There was plenty of pigeons about but as practically all the Company was out every day from 6.30 a.m. to 12 noon it was only possible to graze about ½ the Company each day.

Stunts at ROISEL - Endorse. Amiskey Electric & Rubber Factory. Station &c. German dumps — Shelling & Aeroplanes. too much could be written.

17
June 1917

During the whole of June the Company remained at ROISEL and drew rations from the rail head there. Some teams were also employed on nights work with the RE & took stores up to the advanced dumps &c.

ROISEL was shelled on several occasions, & the railway lines were frequently cut by shell fire.

We were also able to witness almost every day a good deal of aerial activity & the anti-aircraft guns were constantly firing over our heads.

By the beginning of the month the Drivers had made themselves "Quite a Village" of temporary buildings which they called "Tin Town". Some of them were quite comfortable but others appeared to me very much the reverse. The main street was most imposing & had quite a gay appearance with its Caffés & Gardens &c.

During June a great number of guns were brought up all round us & as they frequently fired all night we sometimes got no sleep at all.

Thunder storms were also very frequent and were followed by deluges of rain.

18
July 1917

At the beginning of July, the Company is still at ROISEL employed in drawing rations for the Division & distributing same to the Bde. Dumps. About 30 Teams are employed daily assisted by 20 odd Limber G.S. wagons from the 2 Coy. Divl. R.T.

A few teams go on every evening with stores for the R.E. & one is employed drawing rations &c for the Hay-making parties.

From the 5 inst rations are drawn from TINCOURT Rail head. On 9th inst the Company moves to BUIRE, into a fairly bad camp & continues to draw from TINCOURT.

On 11th & 12th inst two wagon teams are sent out to Bdes & units preparatory to a march, leaving only 4 teams with Coy. H.Q.

On 13th inst Coy H.Q. marches from BUIRE to SUZANNE, on 14th from SUZANNE to MORLANCOURT, on 15th on to TITIEVRES on 16th inst to MAGNICOURT-SUR-CANCHE, which is the end of our journey. H.Q. of Company goes into billets &c.

From 16th inst to 26th inst. usual cleaning up and getting settled.

On 27th inst Divl Horse show at FREVENT in which the Company does very well & takes 1st Prize in the Mule Teams.

The Divl Commander is very pleased with the teams & turn out generally & congratulates O.C. 28th Saturday second & last day of the Div Horse show which was a great success & held in beautiful weather. Distribution of prizes by Corps Commander. On 30th the H.Q. of Company about 9 Teams marches to ETRÉE WAMIN where billets are allotted.

19
/
August 1917

The Head Quarters of the Company which amounted to about 9 Teams all told remained at EPREE WAMIN during the whole of August. We had very comfortable billets & the horse lines were good. The 2nd Cor. Div. R.P. & the Mobile Supply Column were also billeted in the same village during this time. Of the remainder of the Company 10 & 11 Teams were out with the Brigades & a few with Div. H.Q. &c.

The work done during the first two weeks consisted in drawing our own rations, return of the M.S. Column.

On 2nd inst. I prevailed on the 3rd Bde. to take my wagons from Units & collect them under one of my Sergeants who was under the instructions of the Bde. T.O. & it was done.

I had advocated this method over & over again as it brought all the isolated teams attached to Squadrons &c to getters. It brought them almost directly under me & enabled me to institute my own methods of grooming & stable management.

It prevented under officers from doing all kinds of dirty work, in fact in some units they had actually been made the scavengers of the units & did nothing but cleared away manure refuse from the units lines from morning to night.

But above all I was able to arrange that men & mules had a complete

20/August 1917

day off, now & then. The Drivers had a chance of getting a bath & sundry times besides the mules had a much needed day off rest. I was also able to insist that now & anew & [?] had their proper full rations.

In a good many cases this had not previously been the case although I had known this & was quite powerless to put in [?] anything but the mildest protests, which were either not replied to or were replied to in somewhat insulting terms. On the other hand, I must say that there were a few units, and one Battery in particular who took the greatest care of & interest in the teams they had on loan from me, they always returned them in tip-top hole order & it used to be a pleasure to receive, as I did in several instances, very nice reports on & the work & behaviour of their Drivers & for the matter of that of the mules also suggesting that should they have teams from me in the future, [?] same Drivers & Teams might be sent.

The 5" Bde soon afterwards followed the example of the 3" Bde but the 4" Bde though I believe the distances the units were apart declined & collect their A.A.T. wagon teams as suggested.

on a/c of

21
August 1917

On 14th inst. I am placed in Command of the Mobile Supply Column during the absence on leave of Capt AYLMER. ASC.

On 28 inst. S.O.C. 2? Cor Divn. inspected the Company & pleased with what he saw. M.S. Column worked another parade &c

On 22nd inst 2/Lieut J.M. Pinchard ASC arrived reports [joining?] with the Company. He is to be absorbed as soon as 2d Support goes to the Infantry.

August was an extremely cold month for the time of the year there was a good deal of rain all through.

Unless as a rule we [are?] keeping [men?] in condition but their coats are had on of the extreme cold [weather?].

Preparations are being made for the Cav. Corps. Horse Show [near?] Ste P?2 next month.

22
September 19

On the 1st September. The H.Q. of the Company is still at BIRZE WAMIN & as many as can be spared go off to the Cav. Corps Horse Show near ST POL.

It is an enjoyable day though somewhat wet & we had no luck with our entry but were glad to see the R.P. take a Prize.

There was a rumour after lunch that the Vedette Champion Pie had been made by others & many desert picked Cavalry Officers were looking very green and not feeling too mobile for several days after.

As far as I could be ascertained there were no Casualties.

Jeffery Brooks won all the jumping events of the 9th Indian Cavalry amused him noticed a good deal.

Many fellows who had not seen the C. for C. for many years were proud to see him in our midst again looking so fit and well.

The Corps Commander had a busy day putting everyone at their ease &c

Many old familiar faces looked up around & some he had by our surprise which made the afternoon one of surprises & happy recollections.

There was much music and plenty of beer and all voted him happily voting that they had on this turn &c

A. The formation of A.H.T. Coys for Cavalry Divisions was commenced in Sept. 1915 —

They were equipped as far as I can ascertain to carry Horse Blankets in the event of Divisions moving during the winter months.

In point of fact they were very seldom used for this purpose in this Division.

In nearly every instance Horse Blankets & rugs were carried by the M.T.

The H.T trans released carried forage rations in 1915 & in 1916 & 1917. 13 pr ammn & S.A.A ammn almost exclusively.

THIS WAS ON THE MOVE WHEN GOING INTO ACTION —

When in Billets during the winter we collected & distributed wood & Coal & brought in local forage. Hay, Straw, Bran etc etc.
When in Billets during the Summer we drew & distributed rations & forage either drawing it direct from Rail Head or at ROISEL & issuing to units, or by issuing

teams direct & units to assist them in drawing their own forage & supplies either from rail-head or from Bde Dumps, thus relieving the M.T. as much as possible. THESE UNITS (A.H.T. Coy A.S.C.) did NOT EXIST BEFORE THE WAR. Their War Establishment when formed compared very badly with that of Pre-War formation — In Officers — N.C.Os, Drivers Artificers, + animals — In this Division they have done a great deal more work, summer & winter than any other unit in the division —

When attached to units my men & animals were in most cases called upon to do all kinds of fatigue work in addition to S+T. work & in some very rare cases not treated at all too well — Being at the beck & call of every Lt. Cpl in the unit. Mules were not well looked after – & cared for & men were not given time to clean up & groom their animals. I received many complaints from Drivers that they were not given their full rations for the animals. This LENDING OUT SYSTEM WAS FREQUENTLY VERY MUCH ABUSED BY UNITS — who saved their own men & animals & used mine – In the Summer of 1916 we were made into a Water Tank Company, but handed in our Wagons in September & went afresh lot from Asheville to fire up with 13 pd & SAA &c. &c. –

Stations & dates.
Military operations –
Killed & wounded. distinguished &c.
Device on Vehicles a white mule shoe ⋂ — Div. Orders –
X Any other matters of Historical Importance X
Horse Show –

APPENDIX.

Date of formation.
Name of O.C. + date of Appointment
Honours. Rewards. Despatches - + dates in Gazette.
Work each month.
Mileage. Tons Carried.
Vehicles evacuated   NIL
Animals   "   —

Get Hold of Original. + make a
copy.

"A.D.S.&.T., No. M.1512:

   x   x   x
O.C., A.S.S., 2nd Cavalry Division.
   x   x   x

The attached memo from the Director of Transport is forwarded for information.

Every effort should be made for this information to be available when required, and assistance given to the Officer collecting the information.

23.7.17.

Sd.H.Cracroft, Lieutenant Colonel,
A.D.S.&.T., Cavalry Corps.

HEADQUARTERS
2nd CAVALRY D...
A.G.C.
No. 275/1-2/757
Date 28.7.17.

D. of T., G.H.Q. No. 12521:
A.D.S.&.T. No. M.1512:

x   X   x
A.D.S.&.T., Cavalry Corps.
x   x   x

HEADQUARTERS,
2nd CAVALRY DIVL.
A. S. C.
No. 2175/1.
Date 28.7.17.

In order to enable the Historical Records of A.S.C. Units to be compiled in as complete a form as possible and more or less on the same lines, I have appointed a Recording Officer who will visit units in turn and obtain from the Commanding Officers all information which is procurable.

He will then from this information write a history of the unit, in conjunction with the Commanding Officer, and will transmit it in duplicate to my representatives with Army H.Q., Cavalry Corps, G.H.Q. Troops, or L. of C., as the case may be, who will, after satisfying themselves of its general correctness, forward it to my office in duplicate in order that I may transmit it to the War Office.

The War Establishments of 1914, which were drawn up in time of peace, provided for certain units with well defined functions, and the conditions obtaining in France corresponded very nearly to those which the establishments were framed to meet.

A. We ought to endeavour, I think, in the Historical Records to show how these functions were fulfilled, the changes which the actual conditions of War rendered necessary together with full reasons for and a full description of such changes.

The records should also contain some picture of the activities of the A.S.C., the diversity of the work, the conditions under which it was carried out, the difficulties which had to be met and overcome, and the various improvisations and expedients which from time to time had to be made.

King's Regulations Para 1931 lay down the particulars which should be contained in the Historical Record of a Unit, which are for convenience sake repeated herein, viz.

(1)   The circumstances of its original formation.
(2)   Any unusual means by which it has been recruited.
(3)   The stations at which it has been employed, and the date of its arrival at and departure from such stations.
(4)   The military operations in which it has been engaged and its achievements.
(5)   The names of all Officers killed or wounded, and the name of any officer or soldier who has been specially distinguished himself in action.
(6)   The badges and devices which it has been permitted to bear, and the reason for which such badges and devices, or other marks of distinction, were granted, together with the date and authority for the same.
(7)   Alterations in the clothing, arms, accoutrements, colours or horse furniture, with date and authority for the same.
(8)   Any other important matter relating to its regimental administration, such as changes in peace establishments and terms of service.
(9)   Drafts received and despatched, their strength, dates of their arrival or departure, and names of the Officers who accompanied them.

Drafts numerically weaker than an officer's party should not be shown separately specified.

(10)   Any other matter which may be considered of historical importance.

Of the above Nos. 1, 3, 4, 5, 8, 9 & 10 are the most important.

.T.O.

2.)

In order to enable the Historical Records to be readily revised from time to time, it is advisable that statistical information should be given in the forms of appendices to the main body of the History. The appendices can then be added to from time to time by the Recording Officer from information which has been compiled and kept up to date by the Officer Commanding the Unit.

In such a variety of Units as comprise the A.S.C., it is difficult to lay down the exact nature of the statistics which will be of interest for Record purposes, but they should certainly include the following:-

(A) Date of formation of the unit.
(B) Name and rank of successive Commanding Officers and date of their appointment to and transfer from the Unit.
(C) Honours, Rewards or Mention in Despatches, which have been conferred on individuals and the date thereof in the London Gazette.
(D) Work performed each month by the unit under the headings of: average daily mileage; tons carried; patients carried.
(E) Number of solid tyres fitted per month, in the case of Tyre Press Detachments.
(F) Number of derelict vehicles extricated and repaired in the case of Mobile Repair Units.
(G) Estimated number of tons of stores received each month into Base and Advanced M.T. Depots; total number of packages or cases despatched daily to units.
(H) Approximate number of demands received each month in Base and Advanced M.T.Depots.
(I) Number of vehicles each month received into and despatched from Reserve Vehicle Parks.
(J) Total number of gallons of water dealt with each month by Water Tank Companies or Water Lorry Companies.
(K) Number of vehicles which have been evacuated monthly to Heavy Repair Shops for complete overhaul.
(L) Number of vehicles which have been destroyed or damaged by shell fire.
(M) Number of lorries, Ambulances or Cars, Motor Bicycles, repaired each month in the case of Heavy Repair Shops.
(N) Value of spare parts retrieved each month, in the case of Heavy Repair Shops with a Retrieving Section attached.

* * * *

The Recording Officer has now completed the units on the Northern Line of Communication, and has commenced work on the Southern Line. He will then proceed to Armies, etc., in rotation, but it will facilitate his task and enable the Records to be completed more rapidly if Os. C. A.S.C.Units will prepare in advance all the information which they desire to be included in the History of their Units.

G.H.Q.
19.7.17.

Sd. B.Boyce, Major General,
Director of Transport.

2.

O.C., Supply Column:
O.C., Ammunition Park.

O.C., Reserve Park.
O.C., Aux.H.T.Coy.

For information and compliance. The particulars called for by the D. of T. should be prepared in duplicate. One copy to be forwarded to this office, as early as possible, the other to be retained until the Recording Officer visits the unit under your command.

27.7.17.

W.Sutteed Lieutenant Colonel,
O.C.,A.S.C.,2nd Cavalry Division.

WAR DIARY

INTELLIGENCE SUMMARY

Army Form C. 2118.

Auxc Horse Trans Coy
2nd Cav Div.

Place	Date	Hour	Summary of Events and Information	Remarks and references to Appendices
Abbeville	1915 Sept 26		Coy formed at A.H.T.D. & handed over to 2nd Bk Park at 6pm. 102 O.R. 164 mules 12 Riding horses 37 G.S. waggons & one arabarat.	
"	Sept 27		Stables at 6pm as per parade. 6am moved off. Stables great difficulty in entraining some of the mules. All personnel & while & animals entrained by 11.30 am. Train left ABBEVILLE at 2pm. Arrived at LA PUGNOY 8.30pm. First portion met by G.O. I/c Aire upon arrival at AIRE upon.	
AIRE & ROQUETOIRE	Sept 27		Capt Blenard party left AIRE at 6am & march to ROQUETOIRE Camp in field. Rear portion of them arriving at Aire at 9am & proceed to the camp at ROQUETOIRE remainder having finished train for the night; men sleeping in waggons.	
ROQUETOIRE	Sept 28		Camp changed to a better field owing to ↑ weather. Coy split up & tractors & pigeons have had been accordingly. A.D.S. & C.O. Kings visit the camp. Thick mud lines are being laid. About so mules & billets in an empty house.	

WAR DIARY
INTELLIGENCE SUMMARY
(Erase heading not required.)

Army Form C. 2118.

A.H.T.C.
2nd Cav. Div.

Place	Date	Hour	Summary of Events and Information	Remarks and references to Appendices
	1915.			
Rompstone	Sept 29 of		Harness fitting parade held 9 a.m. Inspect & opened-filled obtained for 2 more men.	
"	Sept 30 of		Half coy paraded for exercise at 9 a.m. under 2nd Lt Lyggott other half coy harness fitting	
"	Oct 1st		Eight teams & wagon parade at 8.30 a.m. under 2nd Lt Lyggott to proceed to Olive Rail Shed to draw rations for "B" Echelon - coal purchased at Olive. D.A.D.T. inspects & made a few riders for eating. 2 mules broke loose today & leave camp	
"	Oct 2nd		Eight wagons to Olive for "B" Echelons rations. Very heavy rain all day. 2 mules still missing	
"	Oct 3rd		O.C. rides up to H.Q. N.S.C. One of the lost mules returns by itself. Unless collar chains arrive very shortly from Ordnance, mules will be straying every night, as they can eat through a head-rope in less than two hours. Weather fair.	
"	Oct 4 of		Small quantity of clothing arrives from Ordnance; heavy rain all day; mule lines getting in very bad condition owing to the mud.	
"	Oct 5th		O.C. A.S.C. inspects the coy at 11 a.m. Officers saddlery & reins drawing long arrive from Ordnance today. Heavy rain all day.	
"	Oct 6th		The whole coy paraded at 9 a.m. this morning with long reins. Harness fitting parade for whole coy at 2 p.m. Paint arrives from Ordnance. W.O. Serj Stark to paint the numbers on the wagons. Roller favoured to use on mule lines, no room	

WAR DIARY

~~INTELLIGENCE~~ SUMMARY.
(Erase heading not required.)

Army Form C. 2118.

A.H.T.C.
2nd Cav Div

Place	Date	Hour	Summary of Events and Information	Remarks and references to Appendices
	1915			
Roqetoire	Oct 7	—	The Coy parades in marching out at 9 a.m. as there are rumours of a General inspection in the near future. D.O.O. brings a small quantity of equipment in his car. Order comes in evening that there will be a General inspection tomorrow at 2 p.m.	
"	Oct 8	—	General inspection held today at 3 p.m. by 'S' Echelon & A.H.T.C. A sanitary officer turns up in evening with complaints about the latrines. weather fine	
"	Oct 9	—	Coal purchased in town. weather fine.	
"	Oct 10	—	Billeting acs. made out & rendered. Heavy rainfall. Reason reaches us of the failure of the Nigh advance.	
"	Oct 11	—	C.O. rides up to H.Q. A.S.C. in morning. Vet. officer i/c Div Tps inspects the mules & horses this afternoon. An Officers charger arrives from the H.T.P. which is broken-winded. Complaints received from the farmer in whose house the men are billeted.	
"	Oct 12	—	C.O. inspects the riding school S.S.M. Atchiefe O.C. A.S.C. informs it pregnant. O.C. A.H.T.C. that he had been promoted Capt. antedated to Aug 1st. weather fine.	
"	Oct 13	—	C.O. rides up to H.Q. A.S.C. to see O.C. A.S.C. re returns of supplies. weather fine.	
"	Oct 14	—	Two sections parade at 9 a.m. under C.O. & are taken for a route march for inspection by O.C. A.S.C.	
"	Oct 15	—	Reinforcement of 8 mules & 1 rider arrive at 9 p.m. today. Slight rain all day.	

WAR DIARY

INTELLIGENCE SUMMARY.
(Erase heading not required.)

Army Form C. 2118.

A.H.T.C.
2nd Cav. Div.

Place	Date	Hour	Summary of Events and Information	Remarks and references to Appendices
Roquetoire	1915. Oct 16th		Mule inspection held at 9 a.m. the morning, 2 mules isolated as suspects of pneumonia. Slight rain during afternoon.	
"	Oct 17th		The Adjt. H.Q. A.S.C arrives with orders that S. wagons will be required to go to Aire tomorrow.	
"	Oct 18th		Eight wagons proceed to Aire at 7.30 a.m. to draw rations for 'B' Echelon. H.Q. 9 no 3 sec. parade at 9 a.m. under 2nd Lt. Goett for a route march to Roroque. Receive orders that the whole be moving with Sir Th. mts winter billets tomorrow at BOUT-DE-LA-VILLE. C.O. goes up to H.Q. A.S.C at 9 p.m for further orders re tomorrows move.	
"	Oct 19th		Parade at 9 a.m. move off with Sir Th. Order of march wsd. H.Q. 9 H.Q. K.S.C. (3) A.H.T.C. Units in front move very slowly; at THÉROUANNE 2nd Lt Goett is sent on to make arrangements for billeting. Coy arrives at 1.30 p.m. very poor billeting accommodation. An empty house is formed for Men; temporary mule lines had down in a field by the side of the river. Officers billets very bad. Weather v fine.
Bout-de-la-Ville	Oct 20th		Mule lines changed to a better field - room found for an office, table made by the wheelers out of Bacon boxes. Have great difficulty in purchasing forage vegetables etc. 2nd Lt Goett rides into ST MARTIN to see the Mayor, will arrange to better billets. Unable to purchase any coal in FAUQUEMBERGUES. Weather fine.	

Army Form C. 2118.

WAR DIARY

INTELLIGENCE SUMMARY.
(Erase heading not required.)

A.H.T.C.
2nd Cav. Divn.

Place	Date	Hour	Summary of Events and Information	Remarks and references to Appendices
	1915			
Bout-de-la-Ville Acheux	Oct 1st		In accordance with A.A. & Q.M.G.'s orders 11 wagons 44 mules & 22 S.W. are taken out and handed over to T.O. 3rd Bgde by C.O. Orders come in that 11 wagons 44 mules & 22 S.W. are to be handed over to T.O. 3rd Bgde tomorrow. weather fine.	
"	Oct 2nd		C.O. rides up to Divn H.Q. to see Field Cashier. At 11.30 a.m. at wire arrives from T.O. 3rd Bgde asking us to hand over the 11 wagons at 1.30 p.m. Theronanne — quite impossible as Theronanne is about 10 miles. Our arry & mules & men have to be fed first. The 11 wagons arrive at Theronanne at 3 p.m. & are handed over to T.O. when we arrive at 4.30 pm.	
"	Oct 3rd Oct 4th		2nd Lt Ergott sent to MAMETZ to try & obtain receipts from T.O. 3rd Bgde, weather fine. Unable to purchase coal in Auxquemborgues. C.O. trys to find new billets. Heavy rain.	
"	Oct 5th		all mules & horses got under cover today, none of the barns in very bad condition.	
"			10 mules are billeted in an old disused empty house, to enter which they have to walk up stone steps. Heavy rain all last night & today. Billets found for 20 more men.	
"	Oct 6th		Two wagons sent to Aune to purchase coal & straw stored from Ordnance. C.O. inspects the mules & billets into which they went last yesterday. Start shifting riding horses.	
"	Oct 7th		find new billets for 18 mules. Start marking horse standings. 10 wagons to Theronanne for coal.	

Army Form C. 2118.

WAR DIARY

A.H.T.C.
2nd Cav. Div.

INTELLIGENCE SUMMARY.
(Erase heading not required.)

Instructions regarding War Diaries and Intelligence Summaries are contained in F. S. Regs., Part II. and the Staff Manual respectively. Title pages will be prepared in manuscript.

Place	Date	Hour	Summary of Events and Information	Remarks and references to Appendices
Bout-du-ville	1915. Oct 28th		Heavy rain all day; vegetables purchased for troops at Tanquembergues market. O.C. A.S.C. inspects the billets & horse standings etc at 11 a.m.	
"	Oct 29th		Mule inspection held at 9 a.m. C.O. rides up to HQ A.S.C. Vet Officer inspects mules. Indents etc. for month made up today. Rent of land agreements made out.	
"	Oct 30th		Harness inspection held at 2 p.m. Leather good, steel moderate. Slight rain all day.	
"	Oct 31st		R.O. arrives at 10 a.m. to see if we have any complaints re rations etc. Billeting certificates sent to Mayor for signature & approval.	
"	Nov 1st		Stabling found for 40 mules on the main St Omer road. Spoilt Brett sent to Tanquembergues to make arrangements for hiring some heavy room house standings getting slack.	
"	Nov 2nd		Rent of land paid this morning. No 2 sec is moved into new standing found yesterday. An empty house hired for men of No 2 & 3 sec to sleep in.	
"	Nov 3rd		C.O. rides up to H.Q. to see A.A. & Q.M.G. Got authority from S.O. Div Tps to purchase straw for men & animals bedding.	
"	Nov 4th		C.O. rides to H.Q. to see field Cashier. Return very late this morning. C.O. & Sgt. Brett ride into Tanquembergues to try & find a gravel merchant. Gravel found about ½ mile west of Fillo	

WAR DIARY

INTELLIGENCE SUMMARY
(Erase heading not required.)

Army Form C. 2118.

A.H.T.C.
2nd Cav. Div.

Place	Date	Hour	Summary of Events and Information	Remarks and references to Appendices
Rout de Bethune	1915. Nov 5		2nd Lt Paget sent to HUCQUELIERS to inspect 5th Bgde mules - good condition: rain all day.	
"	Nov 6		Mule inspection held at 9.30 a.m. C.O. rides up to Bg ASC & Div H.Q. billeting certificates taken to ST MARTIN for Mayors signature, weather, no rain.	
"	Nov 7		10 teams & wagons to Wardrecques for coal, weather fine.	
"	Nov 8		Letter received from S.O. 5th Bgde asking us to take coal to La Hieppe meaning a journey of 35 miles in a day. C.O. refuses & refers matter to S.O. Receive orders to send six wagons to the digging party at Ebblinghem tomorrow	
"	Nov 9		C.O. inspects teams that are going at 7 pm to EBBLINGHEM under S.S.M. Michie. C.O. rides up to six teams, Serj Pascoe & sent to EBBLINGHEM under S.S.M. Michie. C.O. rides up to H.Q. A.S.C. & Cav obtains leave of absence in England, starting tomorrow.	
"	Nov 10		Wire comes from H.Q. "leave inadvisable" C.O. proceeds on leave at 2. P.M. by bugler over to Proffett.	
"	Nov 11		Fresh billets have to be found for about 40 mules, as the roof of one a barn in which mules were billeted shifted about 6" over to the side & nearly fell in. Six motor lorry loads of coal arrive from Wardrecques & are shunted by no 2 see billets 2nd Lt Paget rides up to see O.C. A.S.C. weather, light rain

Army Form C. 2118.

A.H.T.C.
2nd Cav. Div.

WAR DIARY
INTELLIGENCE SUMMARY.
(Erase heading not required.)

Place	Date	Hour	Summary of Events and Information	Remarks and references to Appendices
Bout-de-Ville	Nov 13 1915		No mails or papers in today. Boulogne still closed. Three wagons sent to fetch gravel for horse standings. Weather, rain all day.	
"	Nov 14		A riding horse reported in very bad condition. Veterinary given orders for him to be shot. Orders received that 9 wagons will be required to assist the 4th Bgde who are moving into new billets 16th inst.	
"	Nov 15		Hard frost. Boulogne still closed - 2nd Lt Pott rides to THIEMBRONNE & gets 2000 francs from Field Cashier. Orders given for artificers to visit detachment at EBBLINGHEM tomorrow.	
"	Nov 16		About 4 inches snow fell during the night 15/16th. Transport put on as many mules as possible - at 1:15pm 2nd Lt Pott takes 9 wagons & teams to AVROULT & hands them over to the Transport Officer 4th Bgde. Heavy mist during afternoon - roads very slippery. Roads in very bad state, half thawed snow & thick mud. Conduct sheets checked.	
"	Nov 17		No wagons left in - allotton command leaving room in afternoon. Snow still on ground. Inspection of sick mules held at 10.30 am. Eight of the nine wagons sent to 4th Bgde arrive come back during afternoon.	
"	Nov 19		Letter arrives from O.C. A.C.C. saying that S.S.M. Pollitt may be reduced to L.Cpl — AA + Q. G. comes about 4.15pm to see about filling up cavalrymen being posted to us etc.	

WAR DIARY

INTELLIGENCE SUMMARY.
(Erase heading not required.)

Army Form C. 2118.

A.H.T.C.
2nd Cav. Div.

Instructions regarding War Diaries and Intelligence Summaries are contained in F. S. Regs., Part II. and the Staff Manual respectively. Title pages will be prepared in manuscript.

Place	Date	Hour	Summary of Events and Information	Remarks and references to Appendices
Bourdon-sur-Ville	Nov 20"		Nine wagons sent to Lumbres for coal under S.S.M. Itchie, returns etc from Two Drivers placed under arrest by S.S.M. Itchie – drunkenness – Resisting to fall in as escort.	
"	Nov 21st		Pte Jelatin remanded for trial by O.C. A.S.C. – Men washing room made for men at H.Q.	
"	Nov 22nd		Pte Close remanded for trial by O.C. A.S.C. – Both men sent to O.C. A.S.C. for trial. Pte Close awarded 10 days F.P. no.1. Jelatin 7 days F.P. no 2. – Three Boys bicycles arrive from Ordnance. Weather warmer	
"	Nov 23rd		The owner of the house in which we are billeted comes & he has away the stable doors for orders that 16 wagons will be returned tomorrow from 3rd & 5th Bgds. C.O. returns of leave arrives 8.30 p.m.	
"	Nov 24th		Sixteen wagons arrive from 3rd & 5th Bgds, receive orders that they are to be sent to the digging party at EBBLINGHEM tomorrow – all D's refitted & wagons up put in for a special	
"	Nov 25th		Fifteen wagons parade at 10 a.m. & are sent to Ebblinghem under S.S.M. Michie, weather fine	
"	Nov 26th		Wagons employed in fetching gravel for horse standing – Snow following afternoon.	
"	Nov 27"		C.O. goes to see O.C. A.S.C. about the new dismounted div. in which the Can. H.T. Coy is to be employed in taking supplies to div Hd. 12th Lancers Coy 16 horses wagons to cart manure. C.O. refuses.	
"	Nov 28th		Wagons sent to B. No. 3 Baths for horse eng. Brothers are going up to the front – weather very cold and froze.	
"	Nov 29th		Officer i/c det. at Ebbling Lenbachs for reinforcements. Orders for 5 wagons to go to Humbroutorrons,	
"	Nov 30th		Good demonstration held of Jamppen bergus. 2nd Lr Gott sent (as representing) C.O. rides to see O.C. A.S.C.	

Army Form C. 2118.

WAR DIARY
INTELLIGENCE SUMMARY
(Erase heading not required.)

A.H.T.C. 2nd Cav. Div.

Place	Date	Hour	Summary of Events and Information	Remarks and references to Appendices
	1915			
Autole-la-Ville	Dec 1st		C.O. visits detachment at EBBLINGHEM and returns at 11.15 p.m. Order received at 11 a.m. to send 2 wagons to WIZERNES to fetch building material, to take to BAYENGHEM. Total distance 25 miles, return at 10 p.m.	
"	Dec 2nd		C.O. rode to Hqrs to see Field Cashier. Veterinary Officer inspects sick mules at 10 a.m. Gy Peyecl out 5 pm. 1 wagon proceeded to WIZERNES to draw material for repair of billets. 1 wagon returned from J Batt L/a.	
"	Dec 3rd		O.C. A.S.C. inspects billets & talks in accomn at 2 pm of C.S.M Pettit. Pettit returned to L. Cpl. C.Q.M.S. Phs promoted C.S.M. — Three untrained drivers arrive from base.	
"	Dec 4		Three young trained Drivers despatched to base for transfer to England. 2 S/Sgt L/Cpl Pettit sent transferred to Hq. 3rd Sqdn. Mule inspection 11 am. Fresh scheme comes in from O.C. A.S.C. re the dismounted div formed by Car Corps.	
"	Dec 5		Harness inspection Rgtl at 11.45 am. C.O. rides up to see O.C. A.S.C. re dismounted div.	
"	Dec 6		Wagons employed on moving manure & carting gravel to better the horse standings.	
"	Dec 7		Five wagons proceed to Fruges for coal at 12.30. — C.O. rides to see O.C. A.S.C. Rec'd mail delay.	
"	Dec 8		Two wagons proceed to Lumbres for coal at 11.30 am — Cold drawn yesterday delivered to units. No 2 Ae mules billets in very bad state & seems very dangerous. Pte Hardy returned from R.	
"	Dec 9		Two wagonloads coal distributed. Sgt Popgon Card to Div Rest Stat. Weather. Rainy rain.	
"	Dec 10		Dr Richards admitted R. — 1 wagon to Sgt Popgon to Rouhen to dist clone. weather. Rainy rain.	

WAR DIARY / INTELLIGENCE SUMMARY

Army Form C. 2118.

A.H.T.C. 2nd Cav Div

Place	Date	Hour	Summary of Events and Information	Remarks and references to Appendices
Pont. la. Ville	1915 Dec 11		Five wagons to Hunches for coal. Inspection of billets q am. Drains cut to let the water out of the yard of HQ billet. Heavy rain	
"	Dec 12th		Four wagon loads of coal delivered at Thiembronne. Ten men Sergt lc sent to divine service at trench.	
"	Dec 13th		Interpreter interviews M. Coulon, trying to get a new stall for the mules. A.A.&Q.M.G. comes to see O.C. about sending 3 more wagons to 3rd Bgde tomorrow. Hard frost.	
"	Dec 14th		D.A.D.R. m casts two mules for hire at 10.30 am. which are sent to 5th D. U.S. – 3 wagons at 1.30 pm sent to 3rd Bgde handed over to Transport officer. – Two Dr awarded 7 days F.P. no 1 for "being concerned in stealing clothing from A.71's store.	
"	Dec 15th		C.O. rides to Thiembronne & draws 2000 fr from field Cashier. Arrangements made with O.C. Comm. Sec. to give all the men hot baths tomorrow at trench.	
"	Dec 16th		N.C.O's men sent to trench for baths all clothes, saddle blankets, horse rugs changed. At the same time letter received from O.C. A.S.C. saying that HQ can be moved to Pelleghen and Lt Gerets to remain at Pont-de-la-ville if S wagons! Rain in evening.	
"	Dec 17th		Vet Officer inspects myxless horses mallemed yesterday – Billets & no new show weather fine.	
"	Dec 18th		C.O. rides up to Pelleghen to inspect new billets, moving in on Monday 20th act being officials S wagons!	
"	Dec 19th		All vehicles loaded for move tomorrow. C.O. sees O.C. A.S.C. – 15 sank & fr 23 number S wagons left in collateral	

Army Form C. 2118.

WAR DIARY

INTELLIGENCE SUMMARY.

(Erase heading not required.)

A.V.T.C.
2nd Cav Bde

Place	Date	Hour	Summary of Events and Information	Remarks and references to Appendices
Bout-de-la-Ville	Dec 20th		HQ'rs of coy moved into billets at RENESCURE & EBBLINGHEM. leaving 3 wagons & teams at BOUT-DE-LA-VILLE under 2nd Lt Hoggett	
RENESCURE	Dec 21st		Billets arranged for all men & animals – Back horse arranged to man – 2 men granted leave to England	
"	Dec 22nd		Sixteen wagons on duty, fodder giving party – Orders given for mules to be lifted five high	
"	Dec 23rd		Fifteen wagons out on duty – I.C.Q.B.M.S. Harper occurs him of Pegh + St Fletcher from 2 Infy Vet Sec.	
"	Dec 24th		Ten wagons on duty. S.S. Mansfield arrives from Rem – St Fletcher promoted by 2/Cpl.	
"	Dec 25th		No wagons out. Smoking concert held in evening in a barn. Heavy rain	
"	Dec 26th		Eight wagons on duty – stables moved from the prod stables to property stables at BOUT-DE-LA-VILLE & between arrangements made accordingly	
"	Dec 27th		Sixteen wagons on duty – orders received from H.Q. 2nd Cav Bde to proceed tomorrow to BOUT-DE-LA-VILLE. Grooms – arrangements made accordingly	
"	Dec 28th		Move off at 9 am. Capt Powell rides on ahead of column & meets 2nd Lt Joseph at ARROUIT and suggests, who has had orders to proceed to ESQUERDES, meet o.c. Coy there, 2nd Lt Joseph sent back to ascertain if the coy is to proceed to ESQUERDES or BOUT-DE-LA-VILLE. Coy reaches ESQUERDES about 2:30 pm animals put out in a field & men billeted in barns. orders received to load rations from lorries tomorrow	

Army Form C. 2118.

WAR DIARY
or
INTELLIGENCE SUMMARY.   A.H.T.C.
2nd Cav. Div.
(Erase heading not required.)

Place	Date	Hour	Summary of Events and Information	Remarks and references to Appendices
ESQUERDES	1915 Aug 9		Rations landed 10:30 men 11:02 horses — 2 mules cast — one gone to see M.O.F.S.T. at Lumbres orders received to proceed to ESTREE-BLANCHE tomorrow.	
CUHEM	Dec 30		Move off at 8 a.m. some difficulty ascending the hill outside ESQUERDES 2nd Brk sent on ahead to arrange billets at Coy waters at ESTREE-BLANCHE at midday D.E. is informed by a Staff Offr to proceed at once to CUHEM Coy arrives at CUHEM at 3.30 pm. then billets found for all animals.	
CUHEM	Dec 31st		Forage party sent out new scheme to obtained as far as possible — 12 wagons sent to ILLIERS to unload baggage of one of the batteries — not required — return on abrival return at 5 pm.	

WAR DIARY
or
INTELLIGENCE SUMMARY.

(Erase heading not required.)

Army Form C. 2118.

1st June 1916.

Place	Date	Hour	Summary of Events and Information	Remarks and references to Appendices
VAL de LUMBRES	1/6/16		Aux. H.T. Company, 2nd Cavalry Division. Thursday – Return to DROIONVILLE for M.G. Squadron + Rein. Emp. avid.	
"	2nd		Friday. Inspection of Emp. th. vehics by O.C. H.C. 2nd Cav. Div. – Take over Canteen a/c from Ewell.	
"	3rd		Saturday. Watti Trucks arrived LUMBRES station. /2/ E.S. Wagon & 2 vehics. /8/ Small parcels on leave also Mr. Small & 9 pinafore. Boxing Instr. Course in afternoon. Cold weather.	
"	4th		Sunday. No Church Parade, cold windy weather.	
"	5th		Monday. Two wagons 4 horses returned from 11th Lancers. also 1763 Pte. Lanyon. Q.O.H. with 28 days Field Pun. 1. Cold windy rain. – Capt. O. Connell A.V.S. visits sick mules.	

Army Form C. 2118.

WAR DIARY
or
INTELLIGENCE SUMMARY.
(Erase heading not required.)

Month: June

Place	Date	Hour	Summary of Events and Information	Remarks and references to Appendices
VAL de LUMBRES	6.		Tuesday - 10 Teams to WATERDALL for work for M.R. Su Troops. S.O.	
" "	7.		Wednesday. Instructions for 2nd Divisional Supply Col. Cy. detailed to proceed to Train. 6 wagons teams devoted to form base from Line VI de LUMBRES to from Col. at ESQUERDES for orders and proceed to barracks near South of MARIE CAPPEL. Arrive 7pm. Remainder of transport for 2nd Sup Col. from up during the night - 3rd & 5th Battalions proceed by road to M.T. lorries.	
S. MARIE CAPPEL	8.		Thursday - Brownick change flints and proceed via STEENVOORDE to RENINGHELST arriving at 13 hours. Bivouac. 3rd Batn. join with limber lorries -	
RENINGHELST	9.		Friday. M.T. lorries delivers rations. Pte L. Campbell in Command. Capt Palmer. Capt Martin. Capt Swinbourne.	
"	10.		Saturday. Horse Transport relieve M.T. and draw rations from rail head. Light fuel + Sgt. H.C.E.	

WAR DIARY or INTELLIGENCE SUMMARY

Army Form C. 2118.

Place	Date	Hour	Summary of Events and Information	Remarks and references to Appendices
RENINGHELST	11th		Sunday. Starting returns to Brig. Head. daily. Fire was shown in the afternoon. Have bivouacs near town.	
"	12th		Monday. —do— Endeavour to obtain Company's but services refused. Ammo. to square up o/s and hand over to brig. to 2nd Bn L.G. have transport numbers not obtained. Go through to Brig. there in France.	
"	13th		Tuesday. —do— Walk up & eat and not own force since here — return this afternoon on return to camp.	
"	14th		Wednesday. —do— Return to LUMBRES in H.Q. Car with Capt Winstock and arrive about 8 p.m. Lieut de Paule has returned from leave.	
"	15th		Thursday. —do— Square up matters at Bn H.Q. W/S to Pauls and work out accounts. Improved in town friends.	
"	16th		Friday. —do— Proceed to ST OMER in morning upon a H.Q. Dri- information.	

WAR DIARY
or
INTELLIGENCE SUMMARY.
(Erase heading not required.)

Army Form C. 2118.

Instructions regarding War Diaries and Intelligence Summaries are contained in F.S. Regs., Part II. and the Staff Manual respectively. Title pages will be prepared in manuscript.

Place	Date	Hour	Summary of Events and Information	Remarks and references to Appendices
RENINGELST	17th		Saturday. Return from LUMBRES @ 5.30 a.m. in H.Q. Car arriving in RENINGELST at 7 a.m. Our trip from us to which we have been continuous except during the night & the funeral kiss.	
"	18th		Sunday. Quiet day. Rumours of retiring to LUMBRES.	
"	19th		Monday. Received orders to send in wagons & men, at first when change there and proceeds to Ste MARIE CAPPEL there to entrain for ypres. O.C. detained to take down Transport to station. 3rd Battalion here.	
"	19th		Monday. Receive orders to proceed to VAL DE LUMBRES. Gp. Sgt. Major proceeds by Road with his not remaining Waggon and my horse. O.C. proceeds with 3rd Batt; by M.T. Lorries arriving about 6 p.m. Regtl. Company which is still at Val de LUMBRES —	
VAL DE LUMBRES	20th		Tuesday. It is found that nearly all the R.E. limbers wagon Meerens have been	

Army Form C. 2118.

WAR DIARY
or
INTELLIGENCE SUMMARY.
(Erase heading not required.)

June 1916

Place	Date	Hour	Summary of Events and Information	Remarks and references to Appendices
Val. d. LUMBRES. 26 Coluid.				
"	21st	—	Tuesday. march to huik speciall to R.H.A. Ord. 1 uncrewing.	
"	22nd	—	Wednesday. To 5 wagons use returned – Squuin up and prepain to march on flushin day.	
"	22nd	—	Thursday. Mue is left of Company marches to HAZEBROUCK arriving at 10pm. Bivouack in field N of the Town. 12 Tenders from Curelly repain.	
"	23rd	—	Friday. 7 Tenders from (?) R.H.A. upon, unracks for Curelly repain. 29 A.S.C. Strings arrive from B.H.T. depot to upload envelopes	
"	24	—	Saturday. 7 Tenders upon each from R.H.A.	
"	25	—	Sunday. 1 Tender from R.H.A.	
"	26	—	Monday. 7 Tenders arrive fitted with Trucks from ABBEVILLE. 30 men + 15 drivers N.F.A.	

CONFIDENTIAL.

WAR DIARY

of

2nd Cavalry Division Auxiliary Horse Transport Coy.

From 1st July to 31st July. 1916.

(Volume XXIII)

Army Form C. 2118.

WAR DIARY
or
INTELLIGENCE SUMMARY.
(Erase heading not required.) Auxiliary Horse Transport Coy. H.Q. 2nd Cav Divn

Place	Date	Hour	Summary of Events and Information	Remarks and references to Appendices
			July	
HAZEBROUCK	1st		Saturday - 28 cavalrymen returned to their Regiments. 1 saddler 2 farriers & 6 drivers arrived from B.H.T. Depot. Have to complete new establishment	
"	2nd		Sunday. Ordinary camp duties - Fitting tanks to wagons	
"	3rd		Monday. Ordinary camp duties - Fitting tanks to wagons	
"	4th		Tuesday. Ordinary camp duties - Fitting tanks to wagons	
"	5th		Wednesday. Ordinary camp duties - Fitting tanks to wagons	
"	6th		Thursday. Ordinary camp duties Fitting tanks to wagons	
"	7th		Friday. Ordinary camp duties Fitting tanks to wagons	

Army Form C. 2118.

WAR DIARY
or
INTELLIGENCE SUMMARY.
(Erase heading not required.)

July 1916.

Instructions regarding War Diaries and Intelligence Summaries are contained in F. S. Regs., Part II. and the Staff Manual respectively. Title pages will be prepared in manuscript.

Place	Date	Hour	Summary of Events and Information	Remarks and references to Appendices
HAZEBROUCK.	8		Saturday. No. 1 Sub Truck and Punton Tackle with lorries. Road march to remainder of Company.	
"	9		Sunday. Church Parade &c.	
"	10		Monday. Making preparations of Camp Drills	
"	11		Tuesday. do	Buses to Eq.
"	12		Wednesday. do	
"	13		Thursday. do	
"	14		Friday. do	
"	15		Saturday. do	
"	16		Sunday. Church & Church Parade.	
"	17		Monday. Roll never shot. Company.	
"	18		Tuesday. Emerson Batta to Company	
"	19		Wednesday. Roll never shot Company	
"	20		Thursday. do	

Army Form C. 2118.

WAR DIARY
or
INTELLIGENCE SUMMARY.
(Erase heading not required.)

July 1916.

Place	Date	Hour	Summary of Events and Information	Remarks and references to Appendices
Hargicourt	21st		Friday. Hand drills. Exercise and listening walk. Trench. R.E. workmen retaining trenches.	
"	22		Saturday. Saviv in about mine truin.	
"	23		Sunday. Exercise & work. Church parade.	
"	24		Monday. Hand drills. Inspection to. Great to enemy.	
"	25		Tuesday. Testing bombs which have been in selected to. mine camp drills.	
"	26		Wednesday. Exercise training parade. Inspection mine parades.	
"	27		Thursday. Road work. Repairing Trench &c.	

Army Form C. 2118.

WAR DIARY
or
INTELLIGENCE SUMMARY.
(Erase heading not required.)

July 1916

Instructions regarding War Diaries and Intelligence Summaries are contained in F. S. Regs., Part II. and the Staff Manual respectively. Title pages will be prepared in manuscript.

Place	Date	Hour	Summary of Events and Information	Remarks and references to Appendices
Hurionville	28.	—	Friday — Revised upon failure from future Com. Hand duties. Good sporting the old India.	
"	29.	—	Saturday — Troops ordered for Tuesday received to R.E. Camp STRAZEEL. Troops now quite. Troops drawn to upper.	
"	30.	—	Sunday — do —	
"	31.	—	Monday — Hills accompanied with O'fer 2nd Army. They took ships & every movement situations & tracks & fittings.	
"	1.			

J. Connelly
C.E.
2nd Corps Sir Hew H.T. Corps
R.E.

CONFIDENTIAL

WAR DIARY OF

2nd Cav. Div. AUX, H.T. COY.

for August, 1916.

Vol ~~XXIV~~

WAR DIARY 2ND CAV. AUX. HORSE TRANSPORT COY

Army Form C. 2118.

INTELLIGENCE SUMMARY.

August 1916.

(Erase heading not required.)

Place	Date	Hour	Summary of Events and Information	Remarks and references to Appendices
HAZEBROUCK	1st Aug.	Tuesday	6 Tanks sent to 2nd Army heavy Workshops for alterations (Tops to be placed in back of Vehicles) Company Routine — Camp duties.	
"	2nd Aug.	Wednesday		
"	3rd Aug.	Thursday	2 Wagons with Tanks issued to "B" & "C" Horse Battns — usual camp duties carried on.	
"	4th Aug.	Friday	1 Wagon to "E" & 1 Wagon to G.J. Batteries R.H.A., to assist in drawing rations — no withdrawal of M.T.	
"	5th Aug.	Saturday	1 Wagon with Water Tank issued to D. Working party.	
"	6th Aug.	Sunday	1 Wagon with Water Tank issued to "E" working party. Church Parade &c.	
"	7th Aug.	Monday	1 Wagon with Water Tank issued to "K" working party. Usual Duties —	

Army Form C. 2118.

WAR DIARY
or
INTELLIGENCE SUMMARY.
(Erase heading not required.)

August 1916

Place	Date	Hour	Summary of Events and Information	Remarks and references to Appendices
HAZEBROUCK	8 Aug.	Tuesday	Munchin orders and Fort Parade.	
"	9. Aug.	Wednesday	Battin parade timed Camp duties — he was taken from the lines revised form 2d Army (New) Work Dept. out for 6 Swt. for attestim.	
"	10 Aug.	Thursday	Exercise with F.S. Wagon to Fort Hill until duties — 5 Tanks will attend Lip-Hill & received from Ordnance with troops.	
"	11 Aug.	Friday	Exercise attend links & waggon wind camp duties.	
"	12 "	Saturday	Received an attached wagon link at Div. M.Q. & instructed received orders from Q & to exchange links with dipping parties in town as possible.	

Army Form C. 2118.

WAR DIARY
or
INTELLIGENCE SUMMARY.
(Erase heading not required.)

August 1916

Place	Date	Hour	Summary of Events and Information	Remarks and references to Appendices
HAZEBROUCK	13th Aug.		Sunday. Church Parade.	
"	14 "		Monday. 4 hours exchanged with dripping Pation. Inspection of water. N. 4 Sect.	
"	15 "		Tuesday. Battalion Parade. Camp routine duties.	
"	16 "		Wednesday. Small inspection & Camp routine duties.	
"	17 "		Thursday. 1 Team to "A" working party.	
"	18 "		Friday. 2 Teams to VIII Corps for duty. Camp duties etc.	
"	19 "		Saturday. Battalion order read. Camp parade duties.	

Army Form C. 2118.

WAR DIARY
or
INTELLIGENCE SUMMARY.
(Erase heading not required.)

April 1916

Instructions regarding War Diaries and Intelligence Summaries are contained in F. S. Regs., Part II. and the Staff Manual respectively. Title pages will be prepared in manuscript.

Place	Date	Hour	Summary of Events and Information	Remarks and references to Appendices
HAZEBROUCK	20		Sunday – Church parade. 2 Teams & "A" working party.	
"	21st		Monday – 3 Teams & Signing Parties in relief for Teams. 6 men arrived from ROUEN reinforcements.	
"	22		Tuesday – Relieving Parade. 1 Team & "B" working party. Camp duties &c –	

WAR DIARY
INTELLIGENCE SUMMARY

Army Form C. 2118.

August 1916

Place	Date	Hour	Summary of Events and Information	Remarks and references to Appendices
Hapsburgh	23rd		Wednesday. Still firing between wadis Tineh - wadi Ameira - enemy aerial bombs machine.	
	24th		Thursday. Company practice - Wadi duties &c.	
	25th		Friday. Alterations in line future Turk frontier expected by O.C. 2' Army (though with regret). Wadi Camp duties & parades.	
	26th		Saturday. Some firing - firing practice Turks - wadi parades enemy &c.	
	27th		Sunday. Church Parade - Some firing.	

Army Form C. 2118.

WAR DIARY
or
INTELLIGENCE SUMMARY.
(Erase heading not required.)

August 1916

Place	Date	Hour	Summary of Events and Information	Remarks and references to Appendices
HAZEBROUCK	28	Monday	Horse parade No 3 Sect. Usual parades & usual duties.	
"	29		Tuesday. Bathing parade, ditch in afternoon &c. usual routine.	
"	30		Wednesday. Very wet day. Camp in bad condition. Everyone &c.	
"	31		Thursday. Fine morning. Horse lines & hut standings – Camp in bad state.	

31.8.16.

J. Rennie Capt.
o.c. 2 Co. St. And. 10. T. Cy Mtr.

SECRET.

WAR   DIARY

of

AUXILIARY HORSE TRANSPORT COMPANY, A.S.C.
2nd CAVALRY DIVISION

for September, 1916.

VOLUME XXV

*****

WAR DIARY

INTELLIGENCE SUMMARY

2nd Can. Divn Aux. H.T. Coy, Army Form C. 2118.

1st September 1916.

Place	Date	Hour	Summary of Events and Information	Remarks and references to Appendices
HAZEBROUCK	1st	Friday	Am informed that all units think troops themselves are being withdrawn from both training purposes. They are to open on 2nd week. This day stores received round camp duties.	
"	2nd	Saturday	As there is no work essential we left to carry out inspection of mules &c.	
"	3rd	Sunday	Church Parade. Inspection / unspection parades which were received from Brigade Padre on Saturday.	
"	4th	Monday	Inspection Orders parade of Company with respect to vermin and cleanliness — Received instructions to be prepared to leave HAZEBROUCK at 6 o'cmm — this day has been cancelled.	
"	5th	Tuesday	Cleaning up Camp and looking over the Review orders at 8.p.m. that all trucks and to be dismantled from the impedimenta — Everyone who not leave Hazebrouck until further	

Army Form C. 2118.

WAR DIARY
or
INTELLIGENCE SUMMARY.
(Erase heading not required.)

September 1916.

Instructions regarding War Diaries and Intelligence Summaries are contained in F. S. Regs., Part II. and the Staff Manual respectively. Title pages will be prepared in manuscript.

Place	Date	Hour	Summary of Events and Information	Remarks and references to Appendices
HAZEBROUCK.	6th Wednesday		Company parade (- STRAZEELE. R.E. Park & infr train from trenches - 8 am. Reserve who are from A.A. & S.M.G. at 11.10 am had Rifles as not to be carried except me & be re-fixed & inspected. 23 O.Rs. leave 4 approach and 23 Army ASC and parents (-"D" Army were re-inspected of ABBEVILLE. An H.T. Lewis sent to munition front & ALLOUAGNE and billet there night of 7 & 8th inst.	
HAZEBROUCK. 7 ALLOUAGNE	Thursday		Leave HAZEBROUCK 8 am for ALLOUAGNE. & Servant & LILLERS and remain there night of 7 & 8th inst. Bud billet in a real field in the town.	
ALLOUAGNE for HERNICOURT.	8th Friday		Leave ALLOUAGNE 8 am v LOZINGHEM and arr near there in cycle convoy with convoy from A.A. & Q.M.G. with men to proceed to HERNICOURT and remain there until further orders. Accident on hill above Thiennes with SMR TOST truck his leg broken - drove my usual into a serious situation in pulling up and in field and then driver serious accident.	

T2134. Wt. W708—776. 500000. 4/15. Sir J. C. & S.

WAR DIARY
or
INTELLIGENCE SUMMARY.

Army Form C. 2118.

September 1916.

Place	Date	Hour	Summary of Events and Information	Remarks and references to Appendices
HERNICOURT to AUBERMETZ	9th Saturday		D.A.A + Q.M.G. issued HERNICOURT was unfit and gave instructions to proceed to AUBERMETZ and trained to ABBEVILLE. 6 horse-vans Light Tanks and remain a night. Set of horses - Arrived AUBERMETZ and remain here night of 9/10th inst. N.B. Cook was sent to Major from HERNICOURT and 3 men unfit to travel were left up incl. Pierre, handed over to LA MARIE and receipts obtained.	
AUBERMETZ to ABBEVILLE	10th Sunday		Arrive [in] ABBEVILLE about 4 a.m. and arrived at a farm. Remain here night of 10.11th inst. Took over 40 horses and 3 mules, hired over to O.C. A.H.T. about 40 wagons with limbers. Receive instructions to proceed in following day to PICQUIGNY and trained to BONNAY.	

Army Form C. 2118.

WAR DIARY
or
INTELLIGENCE SUMMARY.
(Erase heading not required.)

September 1916

Place	Date	Hour	Summary of Events and Information	Remarks and references to Appendices
ABBEVILLE to PICQUIGNY	11th Monday		Leave Abbeville 9 am arrive Picquigny about 3 pm. Bivouack in Vicomfortable field in top of hill. Supper at 11-12 inst.	
PICQUIGNY to BONNAY	12th Tuesday		Leave PICQUIGNY 8 am and receive orders to return to Q. at VEERUEMONT. Much thangs. AMIENS and near R.A. & R.M.G. or Vicqueminck who informed us to march to LA NUIZIELLE & BONNAY and bivouacs near N. of the Village – Long day arrive in camp about 5 pm.	
BONNAY	13th Wednesday		Receive orders to draw ammunition for R.H.A. and Cavalry Bri. Have temporary dumped to Aux. Amm. Column. Drew ammunition from CONTAY & CORBIE. Worked camp from hill near to Village m/g of ink.	

Army Form C. 2118.

WAR DIARY
or
INTELLIGENCE SUMMARY.
(Erase heading not required.)

September 1916.

Place	Date	Hour	Summary of Events and Information	Remarks and references to Appendices
BONNAY	14th Thursday	—	Remain in Bonneck. H.Q. and Bn. move up to vicinity of BRAY. Most of enemy move up. "B" Battery R.H.A and 3rd Cav. Bn. first to go. Expect to work through. Enemy lines following day. Cold N wind.	
BONNAY	15th Friday	—	Remain in Bonneck. line chiefly move up. Heavy bombardment. Cold N + N.E winds.	
BONNAY	16th Saturday	—	Remain in Bonneck. Heavy bombardment. Small rain. Big British attack. Small parties of cavalry went forward. Day out.	
BONNAY	17th Sunday	—	Remain in Bonneck. Heavy bombardment. Small enemy shrapnel shells. Relieve 1st & 3rd Division. Cold rain. Riding horse & mules unsaddled.	

Army Form C. 2118.

WAR DIARY
or
INTELLIGENCE SUMMARY.
(Erase heading not required.)

September 1916.

Instructions regarding War Diaries and Intelligence Summaries are contained in F. S. Regs., Part II. and the Staff Manual respectively. Title pages will be prepared in manuscript.

Place	Date	Hour	Summary of Events and Information	Remarks and references to Appendices
BONNAY	18th	Monday	Remain in Billets. Very wet day & night. Men went to Bath. Camp very much. Pte Cave A/c his return to the Village. A.V.C. Supp arrived. Partich & Company / Pilkis horse and 1 mule missing. Reinforcements.	
BONNAY	19th	Tuesday	Remain in Billets. Very wet day & night. Camp in a very bad state. No news.	
BONNAY	20th	Wednesday	Remain in Billets. For wet day & night. Camp in worse state. Troops & gun teams into & out of funes into field trainings when there is one till 7pm. He think from 7pmch ruling the night 19.10 and the evening wet wound attacked messes & before he went from dinner.	

T2134. Wt. W708—776. 500000. 4/15. Sir J. C. & S.

WAR DIARY
or
INTELLIGENCE SUMMARY

September 1916.

Place	Date	Hour	Summary of Events and Information	Remarks and references to Appendices
BONNAY	21st		Thursday – Remain in Billets. Still cold rain.	
"	22nd		Friday. Remain in Billets. Improvement in weather. Bde. now to form 15th & 20th Divisions. Field Arty. H.Q. to be troubling on armament this bde. Stormont's now commny. lieut. Major Craig S.S.O. assists.	
"	23rd		Saturday. Remain in Billets. I Grey union in morning but has to rest. Very fine day. Things slopen up well. Arrl. of R.H.A. Camn cars in evening to transfer heavy truck up to front.	
"	24th		Sunday. Remain in Billets. Very fine day. Whole camp station. Feet hills notes with answer Exercise.	

Army Form C. 2118.

WAR DIARY
or
INTELLIGENCE SUMMARY.
(Erase heading not required.)

September 1916.

Place	Date	Hour	Summary of Events and Information	Remarks and references to Appendices
BONIWAY.	25th		Monday. Remain in Bilik. Ordinary camp duties &c. Fine weather in camp.	
"	26th		Tuesday. Remain in Bilik. Mule lines & ordinary fieldworks. Trifles upward stark.	
"	27th		Wednesday. Remain in Bilik. Ordinary camp duties &c. Some rain.	
"	28th		Thursday. Remain in Bilik. Ordinary camp duties &c. Mule lines &c. 7 animals ordinary sick.	
"	29th		Friday. Remain in Bilik. Rain all night. Ordinary duties camp. 3 mules evacuated sick.	
"	30th		Saturday. Remain in Bilik. Morning orders. Camp duties &c.	

[signature]
Capt.
OC. 12th Div. Tn., Aux. H.T., Cy. ACC.

SECRET.

WAR DIARY

of

2nd CAVALRY AUX. HORSE TRANSPORT COY.

OCTOBER, 1916.

VOL. XXVI.

Army Form C. 2118.

WAR DIARY
INTELLIGENCE SUMMARY.
(Erase heading not required.) 2nd Cavalry Divn Train Transport Col ?B?

October 1916.

Place	Date	Hour	Summary of Events and Information	Remarks and references to Appendices
DONNAY	1st		Sunday - Still in Camp at Pommay. Usual Camp duties. Paid men in morning. One horse + his mules arrived.	
"	2nd		Monday - Still in Camp at Pommay. Raised at viper and slug. Camp duties. Route march etc.	
"	3rd		Tuesday - Still in Camp at Pommay. Raised the viper and mice of day. Camp duties. Greene etc.	
"	4th		Wednesday - Camp at Pommay. hot weather. Camp duties +	
"	5		Thursday - Camp at Pommay. Rain. Usual Parade tennis duties.	

Army Form C. 2118.

WAR DIARY
or
INTELLIGENCE SUMMARY.
(Erase heading not required.)

October 1916.

Instructions regarding War Diaries and Intelligence Summaries are contained in F. S. Regs., Part II. and the Staff Manual respectively. Title pages will be prepared in manuscript.

Place	Date	Hour	Summary of Events and Information	Remarks and references to Appendices
BONNAY	6th		Friday. Still in Camp at Bonnay. Inspection of The King's Own hut wards.	
"	7th		Saturday. Still in Camp at Bonnay. At Army Games was to inspect about 60 (Kings Own) - health Brusery.	
"	8th		Sunday. Still in Camp at Bonnay. Instruction to which all 60 supra with mounted staff on Sunday, 4 horses move. Very wet night today.	
"	9th		Monday. Still in Camp at Bonnay. Weather all week.	
"	10th		Tuesday. Still in Camp at Bonnay. Weather colder.	

Army Form C. 2118.

WAR DIARY
or
INTELLIGENCE SUMMARY
(Erase heading not required.)

October 1916.

Instructions regarding War Diaries and Intelligence Summaries are contained in F. S. Regs., Part II. and the Staff Manual respectively. Title Pages will be prepared in manuscript.

Place	Date	Hour	Summary of Events and Information	Remarks and references to Appendices
BONNAY (Somme)	11	-	Wednesday - Still in Camp at Bonnay. Park marching and usual camp duties. Cold weather.	
"	12	-	Thursday - Still in Camp at Bonnay - Park marching and usual camp duties. Cold weather - 5.5.0 arrived in evening.	
"	13	-	Friday - Still in Camp at Bonnay - Park marching to —	
"	14	-	Saturday - Still in Camp at Bonnay. Rain forenoon. Park marching and new shoe nailing. L. Smith + J. Jenkins also 2 mules.	
"	15	-	Sunday - Still in Camp at Bonnay. Camp duties in weather. Matin any eau.	
"	16	-	Monday - Still in Camp at Bonnay. Park marching + shoe nailing. Wounded mule in afternoon - heir du duties. Camp duties and	
"	17	-	Tuesday - Still at Bonnay, in camp. Park marching. Cold weather.	

Army Form C. 2118.

WAR DIARY
or
INTELLIGENCE SUMMARY

October 1916

(Erase heading not required.)

Place	Date	Hour	Summary of Events and Information	Remarks and references to Appendices
BONNAY	18th	-	Wednesday. Still in Camp at Bonnay. Route march. Smithers inspection 4 O.C. Company. Very wet.	
"	19th	-	Thursday. Still at Bonnay. Camp duties. Very wet.	
"	20th	-	Friday. Still Camped at Bonnay. Camp duties. Sports.	
"	21st	-	Saturday. Still Camped at Bonnay. Usual camp duties. Parade. Some rain.	
"	22nd	-	Sunday. Still Camped at Bonnay. General parade.	
"	23rd	-	Monday. Still Camped at Bonnay. Arms parade at 10.30 am. Usual camp duties. Mass reinforcement arrived.	
"	24th	-	Tuesday. Still Camped at Bonnay. Arms parade. Usual duties. Men fully equipped.	

Army Form C. 2118.

WAR DIARY
or
INTELLIGENCE SUMMARY

(Erase heading not required.)

October 1916.

Instructions regarding War Diaries and Intelligence Summaries are contained in F. S. Regs., Part II. and the Staff Manual respectively. Title Pages will be prepared in manuscript.

Place	Date	Hour	Summary of Events and Information	Remarks and references to Appendices
BONNAY	25th	—	Wednesday — Still at Bonnay. Home front (1 section) very weak at present. Green + Camp duties.	
"	26th	—	Thursday — Still at Bonnay. Home front (W's Section very weak at present). Received orders from XIV Corps to send Lt. J.R. Smith M.F.C. home on Tuns Rd to R.A.	
"	27th	—	Friday — In Camp at Bonnay. Green + Camp duties. Lt J.R. Smith leaves for England by 6.pm train from CORRIE stn. leave her day.	
"	28th	—	Saturday — In Camp at Bonnay. Green + Camp duties.	
"	29th	—	Sunday — In Camp at Bonnay. Green + Town guard to.	
"	30th	—	Monday — In Camp at Bonnay. Camp duties to —	
"	31st	—	Tuesday — Still at Bonnay. Usual Camp duties to.	

J.R. Quinnell Capt.
O.C. 2/Col Div. Amm. T.S.G. H.Q.

SECRET.

WAR DIARY

of

2nd CAVALRY AUXILIARY HORSE TRANSPORT COMPANY.

November, 1916.

VOL. XXVII.

WAR DIARY

INTELLIGENCE SUMMARY

(Erase heading not required.)

Army Form C. 2118.

1st Cavalry Division
Auxv. H.T. Company
1st November 1916.

Place	Date	Hour	Summary of Events and Information	Remarks and references to Appendices
BONNAY	1st	—	Wednesday. Still in Camp at BONNAY. Drivers moved camp duties. Lt. F. Pepper received orders for duty w/ Company.	—
"	2nd	—	Thursday. Still in Camp at BONNAY. Route marching, washing day. Horses trades.	—
"	3rd	—	Friday. Still in Bonnay. Route marching - Horse power. Paid Uniform ctr.	—
"	4th	—	Saturday. Still in Bonnay. Horse parade routine camp duties. Men weekly.	—
"	5th	—	Sunday. Still in Bonnay. Camp duties etc.	—
"	6th	—	Monday. Still in Bonnay. Inspection. fell Ammunition & H.G. & F.S. wagons preparation for further move in. Recvd orders at 4 pm to report to Division at VILLE - sur - CORBIE. Started at 6 p.m. arrived in morning	—

2449 Wt. W14957/M90 750,000 1/16 J.B.C. & A. Forms/C.2118/12.

WAR DIARY or INTELLIGENCE SUMMARY

Army Form C. 2118.

November 1916.

Place	Date	Hour	Summary of Events and Information	Remarks and references to Appendices
BONNAY	7		Tuesday. L/Cpl BONNAY at 8 a.m. and proceeded to March route to VIVIER MILL Roulleau to hand over all his Stores and other Ammunition in possession to Captain. This dump was carried out by 12 horse wagons to arrive at 4 de Rigras & S.S.M. Hiskin. The Company left BONNAY to VILLE sous CORBIE and arrived the Durrani were employed in the round for the night. They set tents. During the afternoon & during this issued 1 each Puples to 4 of the R.M.A Pulce to arrive in Company Kits brought to back Area. Total 28 teams. 3 Teams were left behind with the Brownheads Quart. Park and 1 Team with the 20 Bde Artillery. The Company Puples with to move off at 10.30 a.m.	
VILLE sous CORBIE	8		Wednesday. Drivers on 10.30 a.m. After much waiting and arriving at [illegible] ground[?] moved up to yr. Shutter about 11.30 a.m.	

Army Form C. 2118.

WAR DIARY
or
INTELLIGENCE SUMMARY
(Erase heading not required.)

November 1916.

Place	Date	Hour	Summary of Events and Information	Remarks and references to Appendices
VILLE sur CORBIE	8th		Wednesday (continued) We marched through CORBIE and onwards to fields to the N. of it. BUSSY. Route taken was via TREUX – MERICOURT – CORBIE – LA NEUVILLE – DAOURS – Cookers arrived in camp about 4 p.m. and Coys. but our kit did not reach us till later.	
BUSSY	9th		Thursday – BALLOY to SUPPEN via AMIENS – AILLY – St. SAUVEUR – LA CHAUSSÉE Cookers & Company Lorries arrived in the bivouac and Bivouacs arriving there about 4.30 p.m. Rolls having been called and the men fed, had their tea. One Coy was to move from M.G. Schrin handed over to A.P.M. I had dinner from St Mark but Seen.	
BALLOY	10th		Friday. Coy. leave BALLOY at 10 a.m. after their Coy. Sandwiches to warmer "C" & "B" Echelon the 3rd & 4th Return and proceeds to billets at ABBEY du N. of ABBEVILLE. Route taken was via FLIXECOURT – MOUFLERS – AILLY ABBEVILLE + BUIGNY – where we eventually arrived about 7 p.m.	

Army Form C. 2118.

WAR DIARY
or
INTELLIGENCE SUMMARY

(Erase heading not required.)

November 1916.

Place	Date	Hour	Summary of Events and Information	Remarks and references to Appendices
BUIGNY St MACLON	11th	—	Saturday – A very cold morning which turned into a very bright day and the best we have had to march. Company left BUIGNY at 8 am & arrived at N.E. exit of Villers on 8.45 am, via HAUTVILLIERS FOREST – L'ABBAYE – CRECY – WADICOURT – VOISIN en L'AUTHIE RIVER where we are to take up our winter quarters. The hotel Monsr CRECY took was interesting but the animals were beginning to show signs of the hard work & exposure. Arrived at horse lines took over horses from VOISIN about 1 pm and found in billets. We had to pull & push mud to get into our billets which are hard up to our knees, & no bunks, were turn'd out into to hunt.	[sig]
VOISIN en L'A	12th	—	Sunday – Getting into & reorganizing billets. One wagon of team, mules & 6 men detached from the Observation Post party III Cavalry Division.	[sig]

WAR DIARY
or
INTELLIGENCE SUMMARY

Army Form C. 2118.

(Erase heading not required.)

Place	Date	Hour	Summary of Events and Information	Remarks and references to Appendices
VOISIN	13" Monday		Condition of mules & horses & work of the transport very poor. Shortage of limbers. Sent to the billets 4 accommodation from 3rd Cavalry Brigade 3, again 1 team returned from 5th Brigade 6, from 4th Brigade 3.	
"	14" Tuesday		Obtain further billeting accommodation. Inhabitants more agreeable. Wagons & teams returned 4th Brigade 2, 5th Brigade 1.	
"	15" Wednesday		Inspection of billets to ascertain material for repair of same, mainly in very bad condition. Weather day & wild. 1 Wagon & team returned from M.G. section 57th Brigade. Send 6 wagons to Dominois. Leave commences for the division.	
"	16" Thursday		Harness & animal inspection. Overcoats getting much wetted in billets. Weather much colder.	

2449 Wt. W14957/M90 750,000 1/16 J.B.C. & A. Forms/C.2118/12.

WAR DIARY
or
INTELLIGENCE SUMMARY

(Erase heading not required.)

Army Form C. 2118.

Place	Date	Hour	Summary of Events and Information	Remarks and references to Appendices
VOISIN	Friday 17'		Twenty men on duty for different Brigades etc, with Fatigues, Coal & Stores & Wagons & teams returned from D. Battery R.H.A. & Remounts arrived from Base. Majority of animals now removed from tether to picket lines. About 20 Men & 20 Mules still require billets	J.H.
"	Saturday 18'		March of animals. Major General H.H. Gascoigne Commanding 2nd Cavalry Division inspected all billets. All men & animals now under cover in twenty three different billets in the whole area of VOISIN & part of DOMPIERRE. 10 Wagons out for duty.	J.H.
"	Sunday 19'		Exercise. Inspect billets.	J.H.
"	Monday 20'		15 Wagons to FORET de CRECY to draw fuel wood for Brigade, Harness & Wagons. 9 Wagons on duty to different Brigades. Confidence cleaning. Inspection of Harness, washing of wagons.	J.H.

Army Form C. 2118.

WAR DIARY
or
INTELLIGENCE SUMMARY

(Erase heading not required.)

Instructions regarding War Diaries and Intelligence Summaries are contained in F. S. Regs., Part II. and the Staff Manual respectively. Title Pages will be prepared in manuscript.

Place	Date	Hour	Summary of Events and Information	Remarks and references to Appendices
NOISIN	21	Tuesday	42 Wagons on duty. Inspection of Billets. 1 animal	A1
	22	Wednesday	30 Wagons on duty including 16 drawing fuel wood from FORET de CRECY. One new improved billets	A1
	23	Thursday	26 mules rec'd H.Q. 23 Wagons on duty. Send 6 wagons & teams to 3rd Brigade for fatigue.	A1
	24	Friday	23 Wagons on duty. Harness inspection. One or two men with colds going sick	A1
	25	Saturday	32 Wagons on duty. Weather wet.	A1
	26	Sunday	Inspection of billets, Evaine. Send 1 wagon & team to Divisional School at DOURIEZ for duty	A1

2449 Wt. W14957/M90 750,000 1/16 J.B.C. & A. Forms/C.2118/12.

Army Form C. 2118.

WAR DIARY
or
INTELLIGENCE SUMMARY
(Erase heading not required.)

Instructions regarding War Diaries and Intelligence Summaries are contained in F. S. Regs., Part II. and the Staff Manual respectively. Title Pages will be prepared in manuscript.

Place	Date	Hour	Summary of Events and Information	Remarks and references to Appendices
VOISIN	27	Monday.	21 Wagons on duty, Harness inspection. Weather cold & raw.	
"	28	Tuesday.	17 Wagons on duty.	
"	29	Wednesday.	23 Wagons on duty. Inspection of all billets. Harness inspection.	
"	30	Thursday.	28 Wagons on duty. Wagon & team returned from 20th Divisional Artillery, at ORNOY, appear to have had a very rough time.	

H. Hopkins
Lieut. A.S.C.
O.C. 14. T. II. Coy. 8th

CONFIDENTIAL.

Vol 6.

W A R   D I A R Y

of

2nd CAVALRY AUXILIARY HORSE TRANSPORT COMPANY.

DECEMBER, 1916.

VOL. XXVIII.

Army Form C. 2118.

WAR DIARY
INTELLIGENCE SUMMARY
(Erase heading not required.)

1st Cavalry Divisional
Aux. H.T. Company No 4

Instructions regarding War Diaries and Intelligence Summaries are contained in F. S. Regs., Part II. and the Staff Manual respectively. Title Pages will be prepared in manuscript.

Place	Date	Hour	Summary of Events and Information	Remarks and references to Appendices
VOISIN	December 1916			
	1st Friday		Still at Voisin. Local Transport duties. 20 Wagons on usual Company duties.	JHG
	2nd Saturday		Billets at Voisin & Bonspierre. 20 Wagons on Local Transport duties. Horses cleaning up.	JHG
	3rd Sunday		Voisin & Bonspierre. Horses cleaning up. Wet day.	JHG
	4th Monday		Still at Voisin. 20 Teams carrying coal from HESDIN. 10 Teams carrying Hay and other local transport return se. Remainder Company duties.	JHG
	5th Tuesday		Still at Voisin. 10 Teams & 20 Bell +10 Teams & 4 Bell with coal. Other Teams employed on Hay & return. Inspection of Animals with view to duty by O.C. Coy.	JHG

WAR DIARY or INTELLIGENCE SUMMARY

Army Form C. 2118.

2nd L. G. (or B-) Am. H.T. G.

Place	Date	Hour	Summary of Events and Information	Remarks and references to Appendices
VOISIN & DOMPIERRE	December 1916			
	Wednesday 6"		Still at Voisin. Cut on number wheel Winstock. Three trucks & rand Company duties.	M.H.
"	Thursday 7"		Still at Voisin - One Winstock outside re: tune. Param M & Scot - 'Mule Empan' duties - Winstock. Cut & tuny.	M.H.
"	Friday 8"		Still at Voisin & Dompierre. Transport of Coal x from HESDIN. Mule Company duties. Cell sick.	M.H.
"	Saturday 9"		Company still in billets at Voisin Dompierre. Of Proceeded to Sues Front & took mind his trucks and returned from Mule West Tumpen duties - her sun -	M.H.
"	Sunday 10"		In billets at Voisin Dompierre. Cleaning up harness, trophy.	M.H.
"	Monday 11"		Voisin & Dompierre. And ammo to HESDIN, used Tumpen duties. Pte 1st 17 D. St La Bri in his afternoon - hit hay. M.T. run into an escort truck to D.P. at 9 am. I have had it in workshop where opened	M.H.

WAR DIARY
or
INTELLIGENCE SUMMARY

(Erase heading not required.)

Army Form C. 2118.

Aux-H.T. 2ⁿᵈ Corps

Place	Date	Hour	Summary of Events and Information	Remarks and references to Appendices
	December 1916.			
VOISIN &	12ᵗʰ	–	Tuesday – Still in same billets. Cold day. Snow + rain.	
DOMPIERRE	13ᵗʰ	"	Lt. F. Pepper proceeds on leave to England – would over transport & company duties.	J.C.
"	13ᵗʰ	"	Wednesday. In same billets. O.C. Coy detailed as member of F.G.C. Martial. Arrived at Brig. H.Q. 10. a.m. would transport duties + company work.	J.H.G.
"	14ᵗʰ	"	Thursday. Still in same billets. Work + Coy duties. Inspection of horse billets &c.	J.C.
"	15ᵗʰ	"	Friday. Same billets. Quiet day. Coy only 3 waggons on duty. O.C. Inspect billets in both Villages.	J.C.
"	16ᵗʰ	"	Saturday. Same billets. 16 Teams on on duty. Mostly HESDIN for coal. Parade proceeds for Captain's leave to England stopped. Cold frost.	J.C.

Army Form C. 2118.

WAR DIARY
or
INTELLIGENCE SUMMARY   Aux. H.T. Coy. 2 Ln. Div.
(Erase heading not required.)

Instructions regarding War Diaries and Intelligence Summaries are contained in F. S. Regs., Part II. and the Staff Manual respectively. Title Pages will be prepared in manuscript.

Place	Date	Hour	Summary of Events and Information	Remarks and references to Appendices
VOISIN + DOMPIERRE	December 1916 Sunday 17	—	Same billets. Quiet day. Cleaning up generally.	M.
"	18 Monday	—	Same billets. Car tuned every 1 H&S DIN, and	M.
"	19 Tuesday	—	CREEY Forum 24 Team — steam [illegible] (shoring). Same billets. Got to 2 a.m. Shoes, hand [illegible]	M.
"	20 Wednesday	—	Aux. Horse parade (8 horses). Same billets. 20 Team [illegible] went to CREEY, where 3 lorry work. Stone [illegible] (3 Col 1)	M.
"	21 Thursday	—	Same billets. 25 Team horses, horses and sick. Horse parade (4 Col). Other teams were out.	M.
"	22 Friday	—	Same billets. 16 Team [illegible] various roads. [illegible] Empress follick.T. Transport [illegible]. Empress follick.	M.
"	23 Saturday	—	Same billets. Horse Transport Sub., [illegible] horses [illegible] Sub. [illegible] horses work.	M.

WAR DIARY
or
INTELLIGENCE SUMMARY

Army Form C. 2118.

2nd Cav. Div. Aug. 14. T. 6.

Place	Date	Hour	Summary of Events and Information	Remarks and references to Appendices
VOISIN & DOMPIERRE.	24	—	Sunday. Still in billets in Voisin & Dompierre. Quiet day cleaning up and getting into trim for X men. an General + breed Transport work.	M.
"	25	—	Monday. Xmas day. Service. Fine bright weather. Same billets.	M.
"	26	—	Tuesday. At 9.30 a.m. the X men showed no interest in his enemy. Inspection of horses + Equipment. Same billets — General & animals. Same as work upon.	M.
"	27	—	Wednesday. Same billets. Drew nuts & 2 b Teams to HESDIN for Col.	M.
"	28	—	Thursday. Same billets. 21 horses in a Veterinary hospital. Inspection of saddles billets.	M.

Army Form C. 2118.

WAR DIARY
or
INTELLIGENCE SUMMARY   2/4 (Cov. Dn) Aux. H.T. Coy A.S.C.

(Erase heading not required.)

Instructions regarding War Diaries and Intelligence Summaries are contained in F. S. Regs., Part II. and the Staff Manual respectively. Title Pages will be prepared in manuscript.

Place	Date	Hour	Summary of Events and Information	Remarks and references to Appendices
OISIN + DOMPIERRE.	December 1916.			
	Friday 29.		Same Work. 24 Teams out on training duties. Important Orders Published.	
	Saturday 30		Same Work. 24 Teams on training duties. 19 cwt. HESDIN. bn washed.	
	Sunday 31.		Same Work. Divine Service ordered to have 2 motors. Inspection Parade Parade. Men from Coy. Winter ready Cars up.	

J.L. Quinley Capt.
O.C. 2 Con.(?) Bn. Aux. H.T. Coy. A.S.C.

CONFIDENTIAL.

WAR DIARY

OF

2nd CAVALRY AUXILIARY HORSE TRANSPORT COMPANY.

JANUARY, 1916. *1917*

VOL. XXIX.

Army Form C. 2118.

WAR DIARY
INTELLIGENCE SUMMARY
2nd Cav. Bde. Aux. H.T. Coy.

(Erase heading not required.)

Instructions regarding War Diaries and Intelligence Summaries are contained in F. S. Regs., Part II. and the Staff Manual respectively. Title Pages will be prepared in manuscript.

Place	Date	Hour	Summary of Events and Information	Remarks and references to Appendices
DOMPIERRE	January 1st 1917			
	1st Monday		Still in same billets. 4 Teams & GREYS on wood chins or wood transport work.	M.
	2nd Tuesday		Same billets. 25 Teams on Transport duties, mining, Repairing Gtden & billets.	M.
	3rd Wednesday		Same billets. 27 Teams ass HQ Div & GREYS. Coal + wood. Wood beat duties.	M.
	4th Thursday		Same billets. 29 Teams on divisional work. Coal & Brigade tr—	M.

Army Form C. 2118.

WAR DIARY
or
INTELLIGENCE SUMMARY
(Erase heading not required.)

2nd Cav. Bde. Aug-14-T. Gy. &c.

Instructions regarding War Diaries and Intelligence Summaries are contained in F.S. Regs., Part II. and the Staff Manual respectively. Title Pages will be prepared in manuscript.

Place	Date	Hour	Summary of Events and Information	Remarks and references to Appendices
	January 1917.			
DOMPIERRE & VOISIN	5 Friday		Same billets. Head Quarters orderly. Inspection of Billets & Stables. Found a great many improvements had been carried out. Saw billets quite new look.	Mr.
"	6 Saturday		Same billets. 26 Troopers arr. ex Various Units.	Mr.
"	7 Sunday		Same billets. Cleaning up. Bed and meals.	Mr.
"	8 Monday		Same billets. Quiet day. Cleaning up & in general smartening billets. Inspection of Animals by O.C. Sq.	Mr.

Army Form C. 2118.

WAR DIARY
or
INTELLIGENCE SUMMARY

(Erase heading not required.)

Place	Date	Hour	Summary of Events and Information	Remarks and references to Appendices
DOMPIERRE + VOISIN.	9		Tuesday. Some Work. Quiet day. Clearing up and improving lines + drainage. Inspected trenches.	M.
"	10		Wednesday. Some Work. 31 began one a mining shaft. enfil. Wood & Earl HESDIN. Quiet sniper. Some fire.	[sig]
"	11		Thursday. Some Work. Quiet day. Improved billets and trenches. Company training.	[sig]
"	12		Friday. Some Work. 2 Trench Mortars [trials] for ease. Wet even. Rest.	[sig]
"	13		Saturday. Some Work. 24 Trains our band went. Rest men. Company half emptied. Improvement work with wood + material recently received from R.E.	[sig]

Army Form C. 2118.

WAR DIARY
or
INTELLIGENCE SUMMARY

(Erase heading not required.)

War [Cav?] Bri. January 14-17. Ey [?]
1917.

Place	Date	Hour	Summary of Events and Information	Remarks and references to Appendices
DOMPIERRE & [?]ON	January 1917			
	14th Sunday		Snow. White. Cold morning. Ran Feb to snow sleigh. 15 miles. Medical inspection A.D.M.S. at 10.30 a.m. for Company.	JnR
	15 Monday		Snow white. Rest snow. 14 weapon platoon [?] out. Improving block sharpening.	JnR
	16 Thursday		Snow white. Go out to LABROYE towed sled experienced cavalry platoon re. hard frost. 2nd Troop out. Visit HESDIN coal dump.	JnR
	17 Wednesday		Snow white. Snow. Rain at day. Visited to A.D.V.S. with men to morning men shifting machinedate. Visited B Mass. not been to afternoon up TURTTEFONTAINE. 26 Team for duck wight coal for [?].	JnR

Army Form C. 2118.

WAR DIARY
or
INTELLIGENCE SUMMARY

(Erase heading not required.)

2nd Cav. Bde. A.V.T. Corps
1917

Place	Date	Hour	Summary of Events and Information	Remarks and references to Appendices
DOMPIERRE & VOISIN	18	—	Thursday. Some fine. Cold & frost. Roads not much affected tris hard frost. Conditions for transport. 28 Teams on duty. 9 Teams this week on errands with mails.	M
"	19	—	Friday — Some fine. Cold & frost. Hard frost at 11 am. Animals prepared for entrain'g & D.A.O.R proceed to division's likewise. Few teams on.	M
"	20	—	Saturday. Some fine. Inspect Canteen and Wash & troops inspection. Blanks under G arrangement. 29 Teams on on duty. Chiefs else run. 16 & 5 DIN.	M
"	21	—	Sunday. Some Wett. Palmitin Church parade in Village. Very cold. There was fire all day. All woman risen up and strew footballs parade. Troops were wild in afternoon. S.A.P. to gymn. C Rider's front.	M

WAR DIARY
or
INTELLIGENCE SUMMARY

Army Form C. 2118.

2nd Cav Bde. Hors. H.T. Cuthbert

1917.

Place	Date	Hour	Summary of Events and Information	Remarks and references to Appendices
DOMPIERRE & YOIRIN	January Sunday 22		Some work. Medical Officer inspects billets in the afternoon & second cavalry field ambulance in same - they each 16 Teams to Hesdin to each 26 in dark chain horses.	[sig]
"	Tuesday 23		Some Work - Key exercise. Head Qrs, Gds, nos. 1, 2 & Mch. Gun Squad. 23 Teams on duty.	[sig]
"	Wednesday 24		Some phys. Key exer. which some recruits & Reptn. for to HESDIN. 15 Teams on duty, remainder ordinary duties & importing billets.	[sig]
"	Thursday 25		Some Billets. Key exer. skating. D.A.D.R. visited FORTIE FONTAIN to each horses. Par vet being medl. Shortage of forage in g lb forage + 10 lb of hay being horses to local farmers, is deteriorating ? than in very weak. They are down to great deal of work & are extremely weak in also ignore him. They require more forage.	[sig]

Army Form C. 2118.

WAR DIARY
or
INTELLIGENCE SUMMARY

2nd (in. Div. Aux. H.T. Coy) ? ?
1917

(Erase heading not required.)

Place	Date	Hour	Summary of Events and Information	Remarks and references to Appendices
DOMPIERRE		January	Same Weather. Inspection had all day. Motor at	
	26"	—	LE BOISEL. 20 Teams on duty mostly drawing road from CRÉCY Inspection loose. Company Orders &c.	MWS
"	27"	—	Saturday. Same weather. Inspection had all day from GEC - stables. Reports have been in wonderfully good condition in spite of the hard frost, more than 20 teams working unless when the frost comes on. Steam wagon used to run from main pn. 26 Teams nc - All lunes enabled.	MWS
"	28"	—	Sunday. Same weather. Inspection had all day town sech. Meeting. Quick day cleaning up machinery - humans & animals in nice tm s.	MWS
"	29"	—	Monday. Same weather - Inspection hard morning - 20 Teams on duty went over AMIENS - Mean that Coys which will be moved to increase to what appear now to be 5th. Also received authority to increase to War Esstab. of Company by 3 art/feers + 6 Drivers - W.O. Lattre 6.1.17	MWS

Army Form C. 2118.

WAR DIARY
or
INTELLIGENCE SUMMARY 2nd Can. Div. Amm. S.T. Co. M.T.

1917.

(Erase heading not required.)

Place	Date	Hour	Summary of Events and Information	Remarks and references to Appendices
DOMPIERRE	30		Tuesday. Same Billets. Very Cold. Matins to 21 Teams on duty. Some Snow.	MM
"	31		Wednesday. Same Billets. Lr. Pepton gone to G.H.Q. for be interviewed by D. & T. re personnel Carriers for Each July. Some Snow. Mules died during the winter. 16 Teams on duty.	MM

31.1.17.

O. Mitchell
Capt.
O.C.
2nd Can. Div. Amm. S.T. Co. M.T.

CONFIDENTIAL.

WAR DIARY

of

2ND CAVALRY AUXILIARY HORSE TRANSPORT COY.

FEBRUARY, 1917.
VOL. XXX.
===========

Army Form C. 2118.

(No 575 G.)

WAR DIARY
or
INTELLIGENCE SUMMARY 2nd Cavalry Divisional Arty.
Aux. H.T. Coy. A.S.C.

(Erase heading not required.)

Place	Date	Hour	Summary of Events and Information	Remarks and references to Appendices
DOMPIERRE	1st February 1917. Thursday		Still in same winter billets. NCO & superior c/c & changed to A & Q. 631 Thomas him as de. Still very cold. Shoeing &c. 25 horses & men on duty nightly in numbers outside village for his friends Frenzies.	M.
"	2nd Friday		Same billets. Still frost & freezing &c. Our riders spend about from 10. A.M. to 4 P.M. This is very little for the inside lines enemy's aviators to work under. Superior patrols &c on a certain rider.	M.
"	3rd Saturday		Same billets. Hard frost & shoeing &c. Pay day for Coy. 10 teams are on duty at chief mont.	M.
"	4th Sunday		Same billets. Hard frost shoeing &c. Quiet day elsewhere &c.	M.
"	5th Sain Martin		Same billets. Hard frost shoeing &c. Some from mont 12 nights. 2 teams on duty at chief mont.	M.

Army Form C. 2118.

WAR DIARY
or
INTELLIGENCE SUMMARY

(Erase heading not required.)

Instructions regarding War Diaries and Intelligence Summaries are contained in F. S. Regs., Part II. and the Staff Manual respectively. Title Pages will be prepared in manuscript.

Place	Date	Hour	Summary of Events and Information	Remarks and references to Appendices
DOMPIERRE			February 1917.	
	6th		Tuesday. Snow fell all day and until noon. 25 wagons at work during and from other front.	M.
	7th		Wednesday. Snow little. Kin exel whecti wagons on a dul. Pompiers.	M.
	8th		Thursday. Snow little. Kin exel spreting to inspection to little. 28 wagons on a dul. including 26 for wood. LABROYE	M.
	9th		Friday. Snow little. Very even weld patil electric day. Trip under. 28 wagons on a dul. including 26 for wood. E DOMINOIS	M.
	10		Saturday. Snow little. fine a mud. tumbil weld. Supervision for Sir Pomin with 28 Teams on dul. - went wood LABROYE	M.

2449 Wt. W14957/M90 750,000 1/16 J.B.C. & A. Forms/C.2118/12.

Army Form C. 2118.

WAR DIARY
or
INTELLIGENCE SUMMARY

2nd Cavalry Div &
Aux. H.T. Coy: H.Q.

(Erase heading not required.)

Place	Date	Hour	Summary of Events and Information	Remarks and references to Appendices
	February 1917.			
DOMPIERRE	11" Sunday.		Snow fell all day. 4 D.F. & T. Car. Corps Coln. no up to Establishment so spare men given to all units. Clean up & check in. —	M.G
	12" Monday.		Snow fell all day. Fresh men to relieve - Some L.G Teams on duty: half our from HESDIN.	M.G
	13" Tuesday.		Some frost. Fresh men to relieve to relieve. Skin shaving vg. Lubrication orders issued to all units. Chiefs & our from HESDIN; 18 Teams on duty.	M.G
	14" Wednesday		Snow fence. Half cars all day. Lubrication until the Puncle H.Q & N.Z. Station at 10.33 am. Spare the under use copies up with ne go & to Chateau -	M.G
	15" Thursday		Spare Motor. Not so cold any fine afternoon. Arrived at Div. Completion no DOMPIERRE 24 Teams out on duty.	M.G

Army Form C. 2118.

WAR DIARY
or
INTELLIGENCE SUMMARY

2nd (Gp.) Div.
A.H.Q. H.T.B.

(Erase heading not required.)

Place	Date	Hour	Summary of Events and Information	Remarks and references to Appendices
DOMPIERRE			February 1917.	
	16th Friday		Same Wk. Sub to in Kw. Push to Station. Inspection & Team in location orders at 10.30 a.m. 16 Teams pit.	M.
	17th Saturday		Same Wk. — first pull orders etc. Inspection.	M.
	18th Sunday		Team in location orders at 10.30 a.m. Football games etc. H.Q. Team in afternoon. Same Wk. Warm day rain. Sewage drawn up. Burin Creek in the and in 9, 7, & Rch. Pit. Further scheme for transport station in operation.	M.
	19th Monday		Same Ricks. 26 Team during winter from front.	M.
	20th Tuesday		REGNAVILLE Chief in 4 Rd. Same Ricks. 28 Team during winter from FREY front. Raining all day. 3 Team went out.	M. M. M.
	21st Wednesday		Same Ricks. 27 Team delive work to Rwndo & went in Cds. Burin pit sends —	M. M.

WAR DIARY
or
INTELLIGENCE SUMMARY

Army Form C. 2118.

2nd Can. Div.
Aux. H.T. Coy 1966

February 1917

Place	Date	Hour	Summary of Events and Information	Remarks and references to Appendices
DOMPIERRE	22nd Thursday		Sans Boileuk. 20 Teams on duty including 10 F	Nil
	23rd Friday		Sans Boileuk. 24 Teams on duty. 17 drawing rations. Chief F.N. 3rd Bde. Received notification at 3pm that A.D.H.S.T. Can. Corps with inspect Company at 4pm on 24 inst. Spent much time cleaning up. Had to stop entire work up to not return until after dusk.	Nil
	24th Saturday		Sans Boileuk. 8 Teams on lines duty in the morning. (Can. Corps H.Q.) A.D.H.S.T. inspected lines at 3.45pm taking several hours to both find with us spent for Quarters etc.	NW
	25th Sunday		Sans Boileuk. Full day. Work slackened up. Quarters up.	Nil
	26th Monday		Sans Boileuk. Normal transport work.	Nil

WAR DIARY

Army Form C. 2118.

Place	Date	Hour	Summary of Events and Information	Remarks and references to Appendices
DOMPIERRE	27		Tuesday. Some Whizz-bang shelling in various areas. Fine day.	
"	28		Spent morning in organisation. Heavy N to N.W wind. Some Whizz-bang & Bdo [illegible] shelling all am. In the afternoon enemy went very active & put over heavy fire [illegible] to our lines in 3 hrs [illegible] been informed it [illegible] if we any [illegible] front line been moved [illegible] received from yesterday [illegible] (completed) which [illegible] (infilled) & (linen). Shots went well & had twice been [illegible] along being fired... 9 hr it not enough for Coy. No wire previously have been put from L Coy to her but I wish it not be returned on Divisional I have been [illegible] that 3 Divisn at all have seen [illegible].	

CONFIDENTIAL.

Vol 9

WAR   DIARY

of

2nd CAVALRY AUXILIARY HORSE TRANSPORT COY.

MARCH, 1917.

VOL. XXXI.

Army Form C. 2118.

WAR DIARY
or
INTELLIGENCE SUMMARY

2nd Cavalry Divisional
Aux. H.T. Coy. A-B-C

(Erase heading not required.)

March 1917.

Place	Date	Hour	Summary of Events and Information	Remarks and references to Appendices
DOMPIERRE + VOISIN		March 1917.		
	1st Thursday	"	Same billets - 25 Teams on sut. 4 other 20 Teams to LABROYE FORET for wood.	M.
	2nd Friday	"	Same billets - 30 Teams out on sut. shingle wood. but 4 Teams to HESDIN for coal.	M.
	3rd Saturday	"	Same billets. 18 Teams out on duty. 10 to NAMPORT for wood. Coal + wood.	M.
	4th Sunday	"	Same billets. cleaning up harness + billets. Rev. service.	M.
	5th Monday	"	Same billets. Heavy fall from hour to hour. supervised. 26 Teams out on usual for sut. pushed 10 to NAMPORT with wood. On Sund. nothing extra happening.	M.
	6th Tuesday	"	Same billets. his moving. 23 Teams ordered for sut. pushed in to HESDIN for coal returning with wood.	M.
	7th Wednesday	"	Same billets - first teams - 26 Teams on sut. - pushed 10 to NAMPORT wood + 11 Division w/D coal.	M.

Army Form C. 2118.

WAR DIARY
or
INTELLIGENCE SUMMARY

(Erase heading not required.)

Place	Date	Hour	Summary of Events and Information	Remarks and references to Appendices
DUPPERRE	Nov 1917			
	8	Thursday	Same Wlk. Went out march from run to [illegible] Tenis in aft. Forted 14 & 6 CANCHY - CRECY Forest to wood. BOXING & ABBEVILLE.	
"	9	Friday	Same Wlk. Weakened of fuck. Same num. 26 Tenis in aft. Forted 14 & VIRANEHAUX wd. Went to 4 & 5 Box. — Boxen. & ABBEVILLE.	
"	10	Saturday	Same Wlks. Weakened within - 27 Tenis as in aft. Further 21 & CRECY Forest & ENEMY for	
"	11	Sunday	went & Box. ABBEVILLE. Same Wlks. Out with Letters the Rev. at service of re. Matheur of fuck. part of the Company on leave.	
"	12	Thursday	Same Wlks. Mile weather. 26 troops on out Chiefs end timed.	
"	13	Tuesday	Same Wlks. 2 3 troops and and and trans funds a.	

WAR DIARY
or
INTELLIGENCE SUMMARY

Army Form C. 2118.

Place	Date	Hour	Summary of Events and Information	Remarks and references to Appendices
DOMPIERRE	March 1917			
	14th Wednesday		Some difficulty. Keep with the Company all hands took up temp we keep supplies food and ammunition into entrenched area when we were put here. Home made grenade H.E & 4 features — 25 Teams in all —	Nil
	15th Thursday		Some difficulty. Training to be carried on weapons 6/15 sub tank (9 IN) + 6 W Lev. 9 in Artillery (IN) arrived 3 Sept. 24 Teams in that further 9 to tree tumps to work —	Nil
	16th Friday		Some difficulty. Men had three weeks training arrive H&5 DIV arrangement — 25 Teams in aft. Three trucks henceforth in afternoon —	Nil
	17th Saturday		Some difficulty. BAPAUME captured by British — 20 Teams all out —	Nil

WAR DIARY
INTELLIGENCE SUMMARY

Army Form C. 2118.

Place	Date	Hour	Summary of Events and Information	Remarks and references to Appendices
DOMPIERRE			March 1917.	
	18		Sunday. Same billets. Guard 20 Carts from Rations went	
			out from HESDIN & arrived at DOMPIERRE.	
	19		Monday. Same billets. 1) were horse teams forming strength ...	
			work for afternoon — M₅ 825 oats & 610 bran of	
			firm Rations.	
	20		Tuesday. Same billets. Cold hazy. Ordered to send 6	
			mules 1- 5" R. Park at LIGESCOURT & 6 hundred	
			men to same - 25 teams out. 20 LIGESCOURT (M)	
			Cont.	
	21		Wednesday. Same billets. Cold & fresh. Ordered to send 3	
			more mules to 4+5" R. Parks at HABECOURT —	
			six hundred now on train. The sum was 15	
			mules under 6th horse as a transfer with the number	
			available. 13 Teams on duty. Pte Taylor arrived from	
			6" D.Q. m a shunk -	

WAR DIARY
INTELLIGENCE SUMMARY

Army Form C. 2118.

Place	Date	Hour	Summary of Events and Information	Remarks and references to Appendices
DOMPIERRE	March 1917			
	21		Thursday. Same Work. Pack each day. 2 Teams on mtg work to Cery for work to E & G.	M.W.
"	22		Friday. Same Work. Pack work for fork em in N Teams. Eng build to	M.W.
"	23		Saturday. Inform repair. Eng build to. Same Work. Cely work to Teams on mtg work. 20 mapus truck & NAMPONT.	M.W.
"	24		Sunday. Same Work. Cely work. Ruth which day. Running up to	M.W.
"	25		Monday. Same Work. 2 Teams a day. charge work from LAMBUS H.2	M.W.
"	26		Tuesday. Same Work. 12 Teams on mtg inspection. Eng. Relieve truck bleth.	M.W.

WAR DIARY or INTELLIGENCE SUMMARY

Army Form C. 2118.

Place	Date	Hour	Summary of Events and Information	Remarks and references to Appendices
DOMPIERRE	March 1917			
	Wednesday 28		Same billets. 28 Teams on def. school 16 to HESDIN for Coal.	JM
	Thursday 29		Same billets. 17 Teams on def. clearing work. 27 teams which from Cnr school – 3rd	JM
	Friday 30		Same billets. Truck inspection – downwards found in machine guns.	JM
	Saturday 31		Same billets. 23 Teams on def. truck inspection & gas helmet parade & drill.	JM

O'Connell Capt
2nd Cav Div. Am. H.T. Coy. A.S.C.

CONFIDENTIAL.

WAR DIARY

of

2nd CAVALRY AUXILIARY HORSE TRANSPORT COMPANY.

APRIL, 1917.

VOL. XXXII.

Army Form C. 2118.

WAR DIARY
or
INTELLIGENCE SUMMARY

2nd Cavalry Divisional
Ammn. Sub. Pk. Coy A.S.C.

(Erase heading not required.)

Place	Date	Hour	Summary of Events and Information	Remarks and references to Appendices
DOMPIERRE	April 1917 Sunday 1st		Sent W/U.S. - Quiet day. Coming up to –	/W.U.
"	2nd		Monday - Sent W/U.S. Uneventful. Nothing to say – R.E. + W/U. clothing + Boom –	W/U
"	3rd		Tuesday - Sent W/U.S. Order received his company to our Armn. Column. Column not then known – Visit of C.C. (Major Thomas) with transport & –	W/U
"	4th		Wednesday - Sent W/U.S. Then an week to go 6 wives. A/C available upon G.C.W.'s DISCUIT and local up M.T. Column. 6 Temp drivers from 3rd Ran sent on from 'The Couriers'. Hand my he for Pay + D.R.L. driver taken month a at up a Without driver. Column who took is at up a Without driver. One Cara to moved to 15 Cluniere.	W/U

2449 Wt. W14957/M90 750,000 1/16 J.B.C. & A. Forms/C.2118/12.

WAR DIARY
or
INTELLIGENCE SUMMARY

(Erase heading not required.)

Army Form C. 2118.

Place	Date	Hour	Summary of Events and Information	Remarks and references to Appendices
			1917.	
DOMPIERRE	4 Wednesday		Ordnance — Remainder of S.A.A. drawn from RE Reserve Park. Working total of 537 rounds per rifle + 2666. 13% full — no rounds to be in butts.	MW
"	5 Thursday		Still in billets. Morning IP MAVANS at 11 a.m. 12. Programme. The order was put back to 11 further 24 hours. Sunday services in upper storey.	MW
"	6 Friday		Still in Somme billets. 2/ Lieut. St Trepin. R.F.A. who travelled from September 1916 to handed over to R.A.P.M. for this. We had walks. Company rest for church parade.	MW
E. MAVANS	7 Saturday		March in + Inchi Qwestin at DOMPIERRE at 11 am. + travel to MAVANS whire miles in Est [?] plus Rues ar BEAUVOIR. RIVIERE. Arrived in 3 pm took up very [?] + line drew the h Ammis also in each upper. Wide tent.	MW
MAVANS & H.Q.	8 Sunday Easter Day.		Market at 3pm from MAVANS to OCCOCHE's shew Company arrived at 4.R. Echelon at 6 pm. Peace our General + no attacks/ments which were made Town Major	9 MW

2449 Wt. W14957/M90 750,000 1/16 J.B.C. & A. Forms/C.2118/12.

WAR DIARY
INTELLIGENCE SUMMARY

Army Form C. 2118.

2nd Coy. 5th Army H.T. Coy A.S.C.

(Erase heading not required.)

Place	Date	Hour	Summary of Events and Information	Remarks and references to Appendices
	April 1917			
	8th continued		Town Major at OEUF [OEUVRES] advises me to move on to HEM which was done & I arrived there about 7.30 p.m. Had good accommodation. Have made enquiries for Coy. Cars & am awaiting to hear in case did to account received *c.	
HEM	9th Monday Easter Monday		No orders received to move to any destination. With high winds. Remain in HEM. Butt to ARRAS. Commences.	
HEM & GRUCHES [GRUCHIES]	10th Tuesday		No orders received to move up to 1 P.m. Ride out to see Town Major at OEUF OEUVRES who informs me my billets have been requisitioned. In the afternoon orders arrive to move to GRUCHIES, where we arrive in my F.S. & shelter tents up. See orders & want every body there which they did rather than went with. Remain in billets full head.	
GRUCHIES & BARLY	11th Wednesday		No orders received to move to new area SUTT down unforseeable. Heard Cels unmade. Day to M & 2' Col Gris arrives & leaves in up store room and is supposed to find my Company billets in GRUCHIES. Orders to move on to BARLY as we are now FOSSEUX Road my work week there much trouble filling the husmib wanted.	

WAR DIARY
INTELLIGENCE SUMMARY

Army Form C. 2118.

Place	Date	Hour	Summary of Events and Information	Remarks and references to Appendices
	April 1917			
	13	-	Thursday. Ammunition waggon on the road met to GROUCHES, which I think where 3 tons in a very full [illegible] which captured his wheels and caused up everything 6 to 12 inches deep. Company arrived in BARLY about 8 pm. and men spent in very bad weather and Sgd Clark on waterproof sheets under a [illegible] in men's tent.	[illegible]
BARLY to GROUCHES	-	Thursday	March back to GROUCHES put difficult from sticky [illegible] waggon tracks in the road which we in places erected villages about 10 am twin GROUCHES in 1 from. my each, which had remained in town — Settled down in our billets. 9 am hunt 'A' Echelon. 3'Div. Arty.	[illegible]
GROUCHES	13	-	Friday. Remain in GROUCHES and for some of the [illegible] remainder picketed in field. Dispositions of trunks as in good condition as except in so in [illegible] Section which had been attached to 1st Batt. during the [illegible] [illegible]	[illegible]

WAR DIARY
or
INTELLIGENCE SUMMARY

Army Form C. 2118.

Place	Date	Hour	Summary of Events and Information	Remarks and references to Appendices
GROVECHES	14		April 1917 — went to fm. Saturday — Some killed. Very cold stand. Enemies and general clear up. Troops train moved to 12 hrs. & 16 hrs & 5 horses. on 12' report. Tanned to do much.	Nil.
	15		Sunday — Some killed. My each much. Standing up each quiet. Cleaning & Pitting & day. Too much to do much in the open.	Nil.
	16		Monday — Some killed. Cold wind brown. Greens & lieuts to day. Standing my head, 5' trenches from Sgts harris in village with instructions on by Sgts from Sgts Commander to take everybody on fatiguing, which he proceeded to do caused much unnecessary inconvenience to men. The officer who gave the Sgts orders did not specially know his own men & neither he had of what recommendations was required afterwards ones told is much so he was subsequent able to identify a sentence who interferes from Co Capts. 118.000 round + S.A.A. + 1500 hand grenades were handed in	Nil.

2449 Wt. W14957/M90 750,000 1/16 J.B.C. & A. Forms/C.2118/12.

WAR DIARY or INTELLIGENCE SUMMARY

Army Form C. 2118.

2 Lt (A/C) Bri Anne H.T. Ey[?]

Place	Date	Hour	Summary of Events and Information	Remarks and references to Appendices
GROUCHES	April 1917			

to O.C. transport. Between WC_s. Bri_s is in deplorable state. No 1 shed is in use as a dump which was being formed when Corps Supply Rm_s arrived in hopes of ahead of [?] Ton it turns had been previously been carrying 3 x loads of 90 lbs per wagon or 3,420 lbs WC 4 mule teams, which is some 9 hours over hauls to be have been permitted & arrived & alums under similar condition. The mules which had experienced four seasons were in this condition, whilst he added a little corn, and had no sufficient difficulty in standing him up, leave lands. This condition on a whole who enabled him to withstand his external cold weather which has experienced although they were in the open without any cover and had to give up their RUGS to help his Cavalry horses which were in sheltered unable even warm. This was to enable to A.A. Q.M.G. requisition his pier carts I had taken to dismiss. Any animals during his wallet or owner he had [?]

Army Form C. 2118.

WAR DIARY
or
INTELLIGENCE SUMMARY

(Erase heading not required.)

2nd Can Div Amm. Sub. Pk. C. Appx.

Place	Date	Hour	Summary of Events and Information	Remarks and references to Appendices
	April 1917.			
GROUETTES	17.		Tuesday. Were kept hard at work during cool, wind stopping from November to March. I arrived at the Time & Gun Park (?) at Souex Billet. Sent Horse Regs. & R.S. Regs. to LUCHEUX. Got wet & cold. Animals fed and watered, turned in for another feed. Covered in.	[initials]
"	18.		Wednesday. Souex Billet. Weather rather better. Air. Clearing up. Lines tipping animals in front. Greased their skid. —	[initials]
"	19.		Thursday. Souex Billet. Sun out. Spreading sun bath. O.C. R.F.C. (Col. Sask Ervine) arrived in afternoon. Inspected lines &c. Given me dump Ammunition the is relieving your supply trains to Supply Column but have very much not worked for having one to return.	[initials]
"	20.		Friday. Souex Billet. Off loaded Ammunition. Apply for finish & less change fit. Rations with am (??). Received instruction to send 10 Terrain Emplaced to 3rd Park of Reserve with lupein(?).	[initials]

WAR DIARY or INTELLIGENCE SUMMARY

Army Form C. 2118.

(Erase heading not required.)

Place	Date	Hour	Summary of Events and Information	Remarks and references to Appendices
GROUVE/129	April 1917.			
	Saturday 21st	-	Summer Weather. Send men to Scotia under Sgt Pryor linings repair up to kit. Coy from work to 6. "B" Bde for Supply work at LE BOISLE - Parts received.	MM
"	Sunday 22nd	-	Same Weather. Coy from work to — Send Wilk's, 5 MGun Sgt & mid men on L.C. Course — 1 N.C.O + 10 men — local trip marked which duster-up, 3 R.S Burp, 2 Artif. Escort for training — Carrying up to —	MM
"	Monday 23rd	-	Same Weather. Carriers during noting to from Dumfries. Supply 3 Teams for Lure or LUCHEUX. 2 Gr 5 M.G. Coys + 3 for ammunition dump. — Receive orders from D.S. A.S.C. to find 10 Teams to dig with us for Bde as turned PRS. Coy Send out 6 waggons —	MM
"	Tuesday 24th	-	Same Weather. Send out 10 Teams as above to be at Lt' Bde. Receive further orders to send on 3 Teams to 12" Lancers. C. waggon —	MM
"	Wednesday 25th	-	Sunny Weather. Send out 3 Teams to 12 Lancers as WAVANS. Supply on working from BOUQUEMAISON. Group ends to — Each way bus up	MM

Army Form C. 2118.

WAR DIARY
or
INTELLIGENCE SUMMARY

(Erase heading not required.)

Place	Date	Hour	Summary of Events and Information	Remarks and references to Appendices
GROUCHES	26.		Thursday. Same Billets. Cold but dry – Routine Training & usual Company duties.	
"	27.		Friday. Same Billets. 6 BOUQUEMAISON. Vety officer inspects 2 Mules – Cpl Sup[?] went down to AMIENS to give evidence in the trial of Dr TIPTREE, R.F.A. & 21st Inst. Usual company duties.	
"	28.		Saturday. Same Billets. Got but dry – Arrival noticed 2 Mules cremated & DEGOCHES – Usual company duties.	
"	29.		Sunday. Same Billets: Warmer weather. 1 Mule sent to PKS proceeded to Esthuy to study cost & HQ 51DR, Brit N.R. Mons. Usual duties. HE. wearing start.	
"	30.		Sunday. Same Billets. Warmer day. Stores return. Rations Return. 9 am. Usual duties. Horse line not in good condition. Under orders while [?] cart runner in. Little [?] shown. Full. Sick than usual injuries sick.	
"	30.		Monday. Same Billets. Fine warm day. Sanitary inspection. R.S. Gmp Coles and ammunition pack. Is now to O. upon them & move from one to be trench or & J Battery.	

J. [Signature]
OC A.V.T. Cy. ATC

CONFIDENTIAL.

WAR   DIARY

of

2nd CAVALRY DIVISION
AUXILIARY HORSE TRANSPORT CO., A.S.C.

MAY, 1917 - VOL. XXXIII.

Army Form C. 2118.

WAR DIARY
INTELLIGENCE SUMMARY

2nd Cavalry Bgde
Aug 14. T. En. A&C

(Erase heading not required.)

Place	Date	Hour	Summary of Events and Information	Remarks and references to Appendices
GROUCHES	May 1917			
	1st Tuesday	—	Same Billets. Usual stable trumpet duties & team exercise soon & O.C. A&C to FROHEN le GRAND & down return to F.S. station. Te remain with OC A&C —	M.
"	2nd Wednesday	—	Same Billets. I limber amounted to D.A.O.R., 1 Pk, Inspection of Ammunition. Ammunition issue. Usual duties. pages &c. &c. —	M.
"	3rd Thursday	—	Same Billets, Usual stable & trumpet duties. Horses inspection. S.S.O. collected usual —	M.
"	4th Friday	—	Same Billets. Usual stable trumpet duties. Men bu afternoon from camp as well —	M.
"	5th Saturday	—	Same Billets. Fine day, Men chiefly thrown & afternoon. Horse exercise & Officers trumpeters —	M.
"	6th Sunday	—	Same Billets. Usual stable trumpet duties. S.S.O. orders & brigade return arrangement for men & horses took to from LUCHEUX Forest. Fine hot weather —	JLB

WAR DIARY
INTELLIGENCE SUMMARY

Army Form C. 2118.

Place	Date	Hour	Summary of Events and Information	Remarks and references to Appendices
ROUCHES	May 1917			
	7th Monday		Same work. Used Supply station until this day. Ride on to LUCHEUX horse to look at land indicated by S.S.O. Told him on return N end of ground no good for fuel to any width of fencing nature and no road to N. Rifwire near drift.	MJ
	8th Tuesday		Same work. Used Supply piquet duties, hay wire wipers & manure.	MJ
	9th Wednesday		Same work. Loud w/M rested and Rode out with afoot to Prunelque examined 4/16 yrs P.S. men at D. TRIPTREE R.E./R. who was Ill returned to hop. temporary charge. Spoke to ... & 7readly ... me. Item in memo on Saturday.	JM
	10th Thursday		Same work. Issued supp recent scheme - Prunien orders from Q. with up Terms to be of each Aripla & 3 To DE ADE (1 Sr H.Q., 1 Sig Sqn, 1 DE Hqs) + Note loans S. Termen with H.Q. of Anfrey.	JM

Army Form C. 2118.

WAR DIARY
or
INTELLIGENCE SUMMARY 2nd Cav Bde

(Erase heading not required.)

Army H.T. C. [?]

Instructions regarding War Diaries and Intelligence Summaries are contained in F. S. Regs., Part II. and the Staff Manual respectively. Title Pages will be prepared in manuscript.

Place	Date	Hour	Summary of Events and Information	Remarks and references to Appendices
			May 1917.	
CROUCHES	11th		Friday. Same billets. All wagons repaired by Personnel in [?] and [?] 2pm. Cleaning up & putting [?] to move to NAOURS to-morrow. Ration to-day by M.T.	[initials]
to NAOURS.	12th		MARCH to ROISEL Area. Saturday. Leave CROUCHES forenoon & march via t NAOURS with 5 wagons. Arrive NAOURS about 2pm. Came under orders of OC R.H.A. (in [?] & billets in	[initials]
to AUBIGNY	13th		Sunday. Leave NAOURS at 8am. travel to AUBIGNY, via CORBIE. [?] [?] billets.	[initials]
to LAMOTTE	14th		Monday. Leave AUBIGNY at 6am. march to LAMOTTE. [?] [?] [?] [?] [?] [?] [?] & Bad billets.	[initials]
to ROISEL	15th		Tuesday. Leave LAMOTTE at 6am march to ROISEL. [?] [?] [?] about 25 miles. Arrive ROISEL about 6pm.	[initials]

Army Form C. 2118.

WAR DIARY
INTELLIGENCE SUMMARY

(Erase heading not required.)

Instructions regarding War Diaries and Intelligence Summaries are contained in F.S. Regs., Part II. and the Staff Manual respectively. Title pages will be prepared in manuscript.

2nd Corps Sig.
Army H.T.G. H.Q.

Place	Date	Hour	Summary of Events and Information	Remarks and references to Appendices
ROISEL			May 1917.	
	16	—	Wednesday — In Camp at ROISEL. Supply Column drawn away Rations. Quiet day, two men sick.	
	17	"	Thursday — Same Camp. The Company inspected by 31 Division who we proceed. Withdrew their Rations for the Division at 2 am, finished parading.	
	18	"	Friday — Same Camp. Same as above.	
	19	"	Saturday — Same Camp. " as above.	
	20	"	Sunday — Same Camp. Same as above, and 31 Division who withdrew their 10, R.Q.	
	21	"	Monday — Same Camp. " as above.	
	22	"	Tuesday — Same Camp. " as above. Two sick men were running in. There is useful about...	

Army Form C. 2118.

WAR DIARY
or
INTELLIGENCE SUMMARY.

(Erase heading not required.)

Army H.T.C. 2nd Corps Tps. Ans. H.T.C. A.D.

Place	Date	Hour	Summary of Events and Information	Remarks and references to Appendices
ROISEL	May 1917			
	23rd		Wednesday. Same Camp. Have returns for M.T. Stores from ROISEL Station. Ex finished in good time — 6 Coy. Div. Ammunition & MT returns from ROISEL to St Neels is reported to have been unsettled.	M.L.
	24th		Thursday. Same Camp, drawing rations for M.T. Services in mud, from Rail Head. ROISEL.	M.L.
	25th		Friday. Same Camp.	
	26th		Saturday. Same Camp.	do
	27th		Sunday. Same Camp.	do
	28th		Monday. Same Camp.	do
	29th		Tuesday. Same Camp.	do

Army Form C. 2118.

WAR DIARY
or
INTELLIGENCE SUMMARY.

2nd Can. Bn.
Aux. H.T. Co. A&E

(Erase heading not required.)

Instructions regarding War Diaries and Intelligence Summaries are contained in F. S. Regs., Part II. and the Staff Manual respectively. Title pages will be prepared in manuscript.

Place	Date	Hour	Summary of Events and Information	Remarks and references to Appendices
			May 1917	
ROISEL	30		Wednesday. Same Camp. Said nothing unusual. Supplies from Rail head to Divisions. Received the usual empties on convoy day.	J.R.
do	31		Thursday. Same Camp. Train supplies from Rail head —	W.S.
31.5.17				

J.R. Reilly Capt.
O.C. 2nd Cav. Div. Aux. H.T. Co.

Vol 12

CONFIDENTIAL

WAR DIARY

OF

2ND CAV. DIV. AUX. H.T. COY. ASC.

FROM 1st June to 30th June 1917.

(VOLUME XXXIV).

Army Form C. 2118.

WAR DIARY
or
INTELLIGENCE SUMMARY.

2nd Cavalry Divisional
Aux. H.T. Coy.

(Erase heading not required.)

Instructions regarding War Diaries and Intelligence Summaries are contained in F. S. Regs., Part II. and the Staff Manual respectively. Title pages will be prepared in manuscript.

Place	Date	Hour	Summary of Events and Information	Remarks and references to Appendices
ROISEL	June 1917.		ROISEL —	
	1st Friday		Still in same Camp at ROISEL. Employees and drivers actions for the Division from Reid have been instructions issued to units & Brigades to their use. No Horses employed so far. Him is addition to Company duties. 1 Team out Water tank in Dept.	Initials
	2nd Saturday		do	
	3rd Sunday		do	
	4th Monday		do	
	5th Tuesday		do	
	6th Wednesday		do	
	7th Thursday		do — Van been Thirsk — green mini —	Initials

WAR DIARY
or
INTELLIGENCE SUMMARY

Army Form C. 2118.

2nd Cavalry Div'l
Aux. H.T. Co. R.E.

Place	Date	Hour	Summary of Events and Information	Remarks and references to Appendices
ROISEL	June 1917		ROISEL	
ROISEL	8		Friday. Still in same camp near ROISEL rick-huts. Employed doing various actions for Division in distribution. Same to Brigades cunits. 10 $ times employed in addition in company duties. 1 Team w/c went Link M/ch. in dur movement.	
"	9		Saturday. — do — (Retain time union etc)	
"	10		Sunday — do —	
"	11		Monday — do —	
"	12		Tuesday — do — (F.G.C.M. at Morning) M/ch.	
"	13		Wednesday — do — (4 w/c times employed to R.E. taking up materials to trenches. 1 Team for Q.)	
"	14		Thursday — do —	

Army Form C. 2118.

WAR DIARY
or
INTELLIGENCE SUMMARY.

2nd Cav. Bri.
Aus. A.T. Cy.

(Erase heading not required.)

June 1917.

Place	Date	Hour	Summary of Events and Information	Remarks and references to Appendices
ROISEL	15		Friday. ROISEL —	
			Still as before. Court van ROISEL Railhead. Company employed during supplying ie for the Division and ammunition train to Peripple & unit. 20 platoon employed on in addition & hire on Company duty. Teams also working on distribution of rations from 4 to 6 times each upon a given renend of Mel.	Mel.
	16		Saturday. — do —	
	17		Sunday. — do —	
	18		Monday. — do —	
	19		Tuesday. — do —	
	20		Wednesday. — do —	
	21		Thursday. Divion within Péronne, Tincourt & Roisel	Mel.

Army Form C. 2118.

WAR DIARY
or
INTELLIGENCE SUMMARY.

(Erase heading not required.)

2nd Cavalry Div.
Army. H.T. Coy. A + E

Place	Date	Hour	Summary of Events and Information	Remarks and references to Appendices
	June 1917			
ROISEL	22		Friday. Still in same Camp near ROISEL. Rue met. Company employed drawing supplies and distributing same to Horse Units. In addition to hire a Company cart. 17 men with mules hack available from 4 to 6 team employed each upon lettering up more for R.E. 1 Team permanently cut for hay cutting.	Mh.
"	23		Saturday "	do
"	24		Sunday "	do
"	25		Monday " related by G' head qrs. Some men employed on night injuries.)	(One Escort + Village Some men employed on much the work (Rotine am and lens)
"	26		Tuesday "	do
"	27		Wednesday "	do. A good deal of farming
"	28		Thursday " 2 horse inspections held during week.	Very wet week.

Army Form C. 2118.

WAR DIARY
or
INTELLIGENCE SUMMARY.

(Erase heading not required.)

2nd Cav. Bde.
Army. H.T. Coy. A.S.C.

Place	Date	Hour	Summary of Events and Information	Remarks and references to Appendices
ROISEL	June. 1917.			
ROISEL	29"	-	Friday. Still in same Camp. near ROISEL Railhead. Company employed daily drawing supplies from Rail Head for Brigade & distributing same to Units. Trucks No. of Teams employed 30 in addition to him in Company H.Q. with Brit- Lah on Brit - 6 Teams - 1 Team employed with to R.E. When not drawn 1 Team employed each night Hear state line at night in examine lines. 1/m vet. each day. July.	
"	30"	.	Saturday. Same Camp. Routine as above. Coel very wet day -	July.

1.7.17.

A. Russell Capt
O.C.
2nd Cav Bde. Army H.T. Cy. A.S.C

CONFIDENTIAL.

WAR DIARY.

OF

2ND CAVALRY DIVISIONAL AUXILIARY HORSE TRANSPORT Coy A.S.C.

FROM 1st JULY 1917 TO 31st JULY 1917.

(VOLUME XXXV)

Army Form C. 2118.

2nd Canadian Army H.T. Coy A.S.C.

WAR DIARY
or
INTELLIGENCE SUMMARY
(Erase heading not required.)

Instructions regarding War Diaries and Intelligence Summaries are contained in F. S. Regs., Part II. and the Staff Manual respectively. Title pages will be prepared in manuscript.

Place	Date	Hour	Summary of Events and Information	Remarks and references to Appendices
ROISEL	July 1917			
	1st Sunday		Still in same Camp near ROISEL Railhead. Company is employed daily drawing rations for its Divisions and detachments. N° of Teams employed 30 in addition to horses on Company work. Some train are usually employed by R.E. on night trains up to even 3 to 6 trains. One Team attached to into tank attached to 5th Bde. One Team attached to Hay pushing park. Very warm weather – fine day.	Cpl ___ Pbl ___
	2nd Monday		Same as above. Dull day	W.P. / W.P.
	3rd Tuesday		Same as above. Dull day	W.P. / W.P.
	4th Wednesday		Same as above. Dull day	W.P. / W.P.
	5th Thursday		Same as above but draw rations from TINCOURT Railhead instead of ROISEL. Fine day but cold.	W.P. / W.P. / W.P.
	6th Friday		Same as above. Fine day. R.E. wagons not required any more.	W.P. / W.P.
	7th Saturday		do do Hot day. One Team attached to Hay making party returned this evening.	W.P.
	8th Sunday			

Army Form C. 2118.

WAR DIARY
or
INTELLIGENCE SUMMARY.

2nd Bat. T.C. Corps, N.T. Coy. A.S.C.

(Erase heading not required.)

Place	Date	Hour	Summary of Events and Information	Remarks and references to Appendices
BUIRE	July 1917			
	Monday 9th	9.a	The Company moved to BUIRE arriving 9.0. am. Take over good camping ground previously occupied by the 3rd Cavalry Division. Cook-house, shelters &c &c which we found already erected and most useful. Heavy rain soon after our arrival. Company still employed drawing rations for the Division from TINCOURT Railhead. Detach- -ments same to 7 Brigades & Units. No 7 being employed. 3rd One team with water tank attached to 5th Bde.	A.P.
"	Tuesday 10th		Company employed drawing rations for the Division from TINCOURT Rail-head & distributing same to Brigades & Units. No 12 of same employed so. One team with water tank attached to 5th Bde. Showery day.	A.P.

WAR DIARY
or
INTELLIGENCE SUMMARY

Army Form C. 2118.

2nd Cav: Div

Divi H.T. Coy A.S.C.

Place	Date	Hour	Summary of Events and Information	Remarks and references to Appendices
SUIRE	Oct 1914			
	Wednesday 11th		Only 9 wagons employed drawing rations at TINCOURT Railhead for the 3rd Bde. Eleven wagons were sent to the 4th Bde, eleven to the 6th Bde to carry them the line of march. The mules are very fit & looking well & complete turn out very good. One day Water tank team still on command.	H.P
"	Thursday 12th		No teams required for drawing rations. Railhead M.T. to trains going to do S. Eleven wagons sent out with the 3rd Bde. Three to Divisional Headquarters. One to R.H.A. H.Q. One to 2nd Fld Sqd R.E. One to O.C. A.S.C. One to Signals to carry them on the line of march. Teams turned out very well this morning makes a total of 40 wagons on detach ment leaving me with 4 wagons to carry the toys.	H.P

Army Form C. 2118.

WAR DIARY
or
INTELLIGENCE SUMMARY.

(Erase heading not required.)

2nd. Div. Tr. Sub
Aux. H.T. Co., A.S.C.

Place	Date	Hour	Summary of Events and Information	Remarks and references to Appendices
	July 1917			
BUIRE.	12th.	Thursday.	Baggage & supplies etc. This day & the following day were spent getting ready for moving off to-morrow.	Y.P.
SUZANNE 13th.		Friday.	The Company H.Q. & Lines left BUIRE at 9.0 a.m. & proceeded to SUZANNE arriving 4.45 p.m. Route BUIRE - DOINGT - MT. ST. QUENTIN - FEUILLAUCOURT - CLERY & MARICOURT. Roads quite good but hilly. A very tiring journey for both men & animals, owing to the fact that this is really the first long trek (last autumn excepted) that the company has ever done, but men & animals are fresh & fit. Lines quite good but mud-guards & the like the men finished right at the end of this day.	Y.P.
MORLANCOURT. 14th.		Saturday.	The Company H.Q. & Lines left SUZANNE at 7.30 a.m. & proceeded to MORLANCOURT arriving 10.15 a.m. Route via BRAY. Roads fairly good but hilly. Good billets in large farm. Thursday & Saturday Animals & being well.	Y.P.

WAR DIARY
or
INTELLIGENCE SUMMARY

(Erase heading not required.)

Army Form C. 2118.

2nd Can. D.W.
5. Coy. C.E.

Place	Date	Hour	Summary of Events and Information	Remarks and references to Appendices
	July 1917			
THIÉVRES 16.A	Sunday 1		The Company H.Q. leaves MORLANCOURT at 6. am & proceeds to THIÉVRES arriving 1.15 pm. Route MORLANCOURT- SENLIS - FORCEVILLE & LOUVENCOURT. Roads very heavy owing to heavy rains the previous night, but beautiful day for marching. Same meal with the 4th Tun M. yard at VILLE-SOUS-CORBIE. Good billets in the night.	S.P.
MAGNICOURT- 16.R.7. SUR-CANCHE	Monday		The Company H.Q. leaves THIÉVRES at 7.30 am & proceeds to MAGNICOURT-SUR-CANCHE arriving 1.45 p.m. Route HALLOY - LUCHEUX - IVERGNY. Roads good but hilly. Mules going strong & well. Have had no trouble at all with them on the whole march though pulling big loads. Billets tres not very good & in a very limited space.	S.P.

Army Form C. 2118.

WAR DIARY
or
INTELLIGENCE SUMMARY.

2nd Cav. Div.
Divn. H.T. Coy. A.S.C.

(Erase heading not required.)

Place	Date	Hour	Summary of Events and Information	Remarks and references to Appendices
HEMICOURT SUR-CANCHE	July (17)			
	Tuesday 17th		Exercise & cleaning up generally. One wagon returned from 2nd Field Squadron. Fine day.	Ap. P. 1
"	18th		Exercise & cleaning up. One wagon returned from O.C. A.S.C.	Ap. P. 1
"	Thursday 19th		If not from O.C. R.H.A. Wet day (Exercise & cleaning up camp which is rather wet & muddy after the rain. Troops inspection	Ap. 1
"	Friday 20th		That required 167 duty men to each Brigade. H.Q. Exercise & Animal Inspection. Sent 21 men on leave to England these men being temporily replaced by cavalry men from each Brigade	Ap. P. 1
"	Saturday 21st		Exercise & Camps Inspection. None lines drying fairly well. Fine day.	Ap. P. 1
"	Sunday 22nd		Exercise & same as above. One team on duty round the	Ap. P. 1
"	Monday 23rd		Exercise & camps inspection. Harness inspection. Fine day Brigade.	Ap. P. 1

WAR DIARY
or
INTELLIGENCE SUMMARY.

(Erase heading not required.)

Army Form C. 2118.

Enel. Cer No. 1.
24 to 31.7. Coy. O.S.C.

Place	Date	Hour	Summary of Events and Information	Remarks and references to Appendices
	July 1917			
AGNICOURT SUR-CANCHE	24th		Tuesday. Exercise & Camp inspection. Nine men sent off on leave to England. Fine day.	App. I
"	25th		Wednesday. Exercise & General Camp work. Fine day.	App I / App II
"	26th		Thursday. do	
"	27th		Friday. Exercise & Camp duties. Fine day to Divisional Horse Show. Company Gun win First Prize for Post Mule Team.	App.
"	28		Saturday. Exercise & Camp duties. Second day of Divisional Horse Show. Presentation of Prizes. Divisional Commander Major General N.H. Greely, CMG, CB, DSO, very kindly congratulated Company Cmdr on his Turn out. One Wagon Team entered Gen E. Regt RHA.	App.
"	29		Sunday. General & Company duties. Packing up kit & moving to going into billets at ESTRÉE WAMIN in lorries. Very hot day.	App.
ESTRÉE WAMIN	30		Monday. Had Ruthen & Company moved from MAGNICOURT to ESTRÉE WAMIN take up billets here. Very hot morning. Move completed 1 pm.	App.

Army Form C. 2118.

WAR DIARY
or
INTELLIGENCE SUMMARY.

2nd Can. Bri.
Aux. 14. T. C. A&C

(Erase heading not required.)

Place	Date	Hour	Summary of Events and Information	Remarks and references to Appendices
ETRÉE WAMIN	31st		July 1917	
			Tuesday. Cleaning up and getting settled in new billets.	2 M/T
	31.7.17.			
			[signature] Capt.	
			O.C. 2nd Can Bri, Aux. 14 T. C. A&C	

Vol 14

Confidential

War Diary

of

2nd Corps Dep't Auxiliary Horse Transport Coy A.S.C.

from 1st August 1917 to 31st August 1917

Antwerp XXXVI

WAR DIARY
INTELLIGENCE SUMMARY

Army Form C. 2118.

2/Lt. Carley Spencer
Aux. H.T. Co., A.S.C.

Place	Date	Hour	Summary of Events and Information	Remarks and references to Appendices
ETRÉE WAMIN	AUGUST - 1917			
ETRÉE WAMIN	1st	-	Wednesday - Some Wks at ETRÉE WAMIN. 37 Wagons are still out on duty attached to the Various units in the Division to manage them in drawing their supplies. 8 Wagons are with F.S. H.Q. of the enemy - Three are employed in drawing our own rations &c to From this Middle Supply Column which we are in the same Village. Part of the Company at EXPM M.T. been to deliver rations from this side. Very wet weather.	
do	2nd	-	Thursday. Same Wks. - Have 1 Sgr. T.O. & Pets. & Pets. 8 Pets. collecting all my 11 Wagons refering them with his Charge of him T.O. - This is a reserve never satisfactory arrangement for man. by War.	PM
do	3rd	-	Friday. Same Wks. Wind Camp and other dutis. Very wet weather - - do -	PM
do	4th	-	Saturday - Some Wks. - - do -	PM

WAR DIARY
or
INTELLIGENCE SUMMARY.

(Erase heading not required.)

Army Form C. 2118.

2nd Cavalry Divisional
Aux. H.T. Coy, A.S.C.

Place	Date	Hour	Summary of Events and Information	Remarks and references to Appendices
			August 1917.	
ETREE-WAMIN	5		Sunday. Saw Wilks, T.O. 5 Brigade, accompanied him down unit. Either sir or T.O. I send him a Sgt't opts and train up to help him along. Usual camp duties and weekly inspection.	
"	6		Monday. Saw Wilks. Guns having gone to Drean for a transfer to his default. He is also 2 hrs absent off leave, particulars taken up to O.C. A.S.C. orders to out. Usual camp company duties. Fine hot day.	
"	7		Tuesday. Saw Wilks. Usual camp company duties. Weather fine, hot dull.	
"	8		Wednesday. Saw Wilks; Usual camp company duties. Warm + fine during a.m. + ...	

WAR DIARY
INTELLIGENCE SUMMARY

Army Form C. 2118.

2nd Cav. Bde.
Aux. H.T. Coy.

Place	Date	Hour	Summary of Events and Information	Remarks and references to Appendices
ETREE WAMIN	August 1917			
	Thursday 9th	—	Same billets. Usual duties — boys of the town ran on W.O. Reynolds, & Pipes returned to leave & England	M
	Friday 10th	—	Same billets &c. Horse Camps & Company duties. On the whole has a bad stack of arms to work unused to do on cane fields in them months	M
	Saturday 11th	—	Same billets &c. Usual Camps & Company duties. Fruit cup & suppers also were room.	M
	Sunday 12th	—	Same billets. Church parade. Chinese turned in Camp & Company duties, free day. Men able to leave lines & Supply Column was not able to leave their own lines but Murphy's. Also leaving with reinforcements. Capt J.H. BREBNER rejoins Bn at the Base on Demobilisation of this Company to attached pending absorption of Company this stamp & Mobile Supply Column. Orders to be attached to Capt AYLMER, a been from 15th to 26th Aug 17.	M

WAR DIARY or INTELLIGENCE SUMMARY

Army Form C. 2118.

2nd Cavalry Divisional Aux. H.T. Coy. A.S.C.

August 1917

Place	Date	Hour	Summary of Events and Information	Remarks and references to Appendices
ETREE WAMIN	13th Monday		Same billets at ETREE WAMIN. Usual Camp & Company duties. 36 teams are still out with Brigades & Div. H.Q. 1 Team with D.E.A.P.C. Capt AYLMER O.C. Mobile Supply Column gone on leave & Lieut sinnis relies O.C. of the H.T. Acquirement as at rice week to put into readiness for M.S. Column & for a future visit by some of the staber. P.S. trappers.	App
"	14th Tuesday		Same billets. Usual Camp & Company duties. Review wires & troubles. Coy Corps. Horse Show is an event all — Mobile Supply Column 2 normal visit — put been supor standings. Subasions & haven at M.S. Column. 5 or 6 hours we found with riders & dismounted for exting on our our lines ap. A number & other quils hurdrills by draught proteins have manores hes P.O.E. Dr. in imper sort with —	App

Army Form C. 2118.

WAR DIARY
or
INTELLIGENCE SUMMARY.
(Erase heading not required.)

3rd Cavalry Div.
Aux. H.T. Coy. A.S.C.

Place	Date	Hour	Summary of Events and Information	Remarks and references to Appendices
	August 1917			
ETRIBI NAMIN	15th		Wednesday — Same Rilieks — Usual Coy & Company Hq — Saddle & Harness inspection — Again inspect Teams of Mobile Supply Column — Find shoeing and nails fairly in 3rd Bde. Off. Horses 20 Answers in fairly usual for wear — Take steps to improve conditions generally. Received Order that P.S.O. Div. while inspect Aux. H.T. Mob. Supply Column on Monday 20 inst — Return to be drawn by M.T. on 19th & 20th inst.	M.L.
"	16th		Thursday — Same Billets — Usual Coy & Company Parades — Inspect Mobile Supply Column turn in Supper etc turn up.	M.L.
"	17th		Friday — Same Billets — Usual Coy & Company Parades — Hold a Marching Order Parade of Mobile Supply Column — fit to harness & saddlery which is in a very fair & useful serviceable state.	M.L.

WAR DIARY
or
INTELLIGENCE SUMMARY.

Army Form C. 2118.

2nd Can. Divl. Aux. H.T. Coy.

Place	Date	Hour	Summary of Events and Information	Remarks and references to Appendices
ETREE WAMIN.	August 1917			
	18th		Saturday. Usual Company duties to impress — ing own Company in unloading Column. General clean up London harness inspections.	AHL
"	19th		Sunday. Usual Company duties. All hands cleaning up for an inspection of R.O.C. by an [?].	AHL
"	20th		Monday. Usual M.T. & Mobile supply Column drawn behind 4 M.T. Inspection of Aux. H.T. & Mobile supply Column by R.O.C. 2nd Can. Divn. who was pleased with the turn out of the Aux H.T. Coy. after informed O.C. Company that he was quite satisfied with the turn out & hoped that they will (the Company) who were with the M.S. units were in the same condition. He also agreed with the suggestion of having all our wagons in July with figures when ever possible. Replaced under the Adj T.O. A Corporal & mirror trucks his driver when enroute [?]	AHL

WAR DIARY
or
INTELLIGENCE SUMMARY.

Army Form C. 2118.

2nd Can. Div. Aux. H.T. Coy.

Place	Date	Hour	Summary of Events and Information	Remarks and references to Appendices
ETRIES NAMIN	August 1917			
	20th Monday		(Continued) The G.O.C. Sir. Wm. orr was with me walk in from one of the Mob. Supply Columns & they are indeed in a fine shape again.	July
"	21st Tuesday		Same billets – Horse Company duties' parades. The A.D.V.S. inspected all horses of the Horse Supply Column & recommended 7 to entrain, + 11 to be exchanged in public remount mule for 150 mule. In the evening I went through the whole of the horses standing of the M.S.C. (60 double seks) + made an list to achieve proper fit entire in own and + winter work.	July
"	22nd Wednesday		Same billets – Horse Company duties' parades – 2/Lieut. T.H. Bresnan A.S.C. sent to report to H.Q. 4th Co. Company. He is attached pending absorption – Mob. S. Column 3rd Bde. is inspected by B. Gen. 3rd Bde.	July

WAR DIARY or INTELLIGENCE SUMMARY

Army Form C. 2118.

2nd Cav. Bde.
Aus. 4. T. Cuy.

(Erase heading not required.)

Place	Date	Hour	Summary of Events and Information	Remarks and references to Appendices
	August 1916			
ETREE WAMIN	23	Thursday	Same Billets. Usual Camp duties & parades. Pte Gun. & Pole interest in session the M&S Column.	W/L
	24	Friday	Same Billets. Usual Camp duties & parades. Lt Gen L. Bale inspected in action the M&S Column.	W/L
	25	Saturday	Same Billets. Usual Camp duties & parades. General Cummin up the Mob. S. Column continued.	W/L
	26	Sunday	Same billets. Usual Camp duties & parades. Capt Cuplin O.C. M.S. Supply Column returned — I went to visit back to him — very cold sunset etc.	W/L
	27	Monday	Same billets. Usual Camp duties & parades. Much wind storm. Camp home line.	W/L

Army Form C. 2118.

WAR DIARY
or
INTELLIGENCE SUMMARY.

(Erase heading not required.)

2d Can Div

Aux H.T. Supply Column H.Q.

Place	Date	Hour	Summary of Events and Information	Remarks and references to Appendices
			— August 1917 —	
TRÉE WAMIN	28.	Tuesday	Same billets. Usual Camp routine within and road run — took all horses down to the river when off to within had up horses. Trans. Co. Col. Coates, hour saw which lithe place in Country and who down well —	M
	29.	Wednesday	Same billets — usual Camp duties. Pierre — fly worm all rain. Hours on a tide in history exhibits but had back me very tired in s/o of the extreme cold. Fr	M
	30.	Thursday	August — Same billets — usual Camp duties — Standings fairly clean.	M
	31.	Friday	Same billets — usual Camp duties. Horses to parade — send on made down and to paradise for horse show.	YMK

3.9.17.

O. R. Cornell Capt.
OC
Aux Can, Div, Aux H.T. Cy ABC

Vol 15

Confidential

War Diary

of

2ND Cav Div Anx A.I. Coy A.I.C

From 1/9/17 To 30/9/17

Volume XXXVII

Army Form C. 2118.

WAR DIARY
or
INTELLIGENCE SUMMARY.
(Erase heading not required.)

2nd Cavalry Divisional Aux. H.T. Coy.

Place	Date	Hour	Summary of Events and Information	Remarks and references to Appendices
ETREE WAMIN.	September 1917			
	1st	Saturday	Same billets. Usual Camp duties. Cars. Corps. Horse Show at St. POL. Enjoyable day but rather wet.	
"	2nd	Sunday	Same billets. Usual duties & parades. Lieut. F. Pepper leaves on transfer to Infantry with order to report at Rouen by civil.	
"	3rd	Monday	Same billets. Usual duties & parades. Sanitary Inspection of billets & lines by A.D.M.S. 2nd Cav. Div. at 12 noon, who was satisfied with all he saw. Rather hot weather.	
"	4th	Tuesday	Same billets. Usual duties & parades. Several eleven up & inspection by O.C. company of animals thrown in sickness for Inspection of A.D. F.S.T. Cav. Corps on Thursday.	
"	5th	Wednesday	Same billets. Usual duties & parades. M.T. Lorries on return to O.C. Company unpack arrival of 20 Set. which are also for the unit. Inspection in manner the armourer etc being opened on to Equipment with.	

Army Form C. 2118.

WAR DIARY
or
INTELLIGENCE SUMMARY.

2nd Corps Sig.
Aug H.T. Coy H.Q.

(Erase heading not required.)

Place	Date	Hour	Summary of Events and Information	Remarks and references to Appendices
	September 1917.			
ETREE	6.	Thursday	Same billets. General Cunning up F.A.D F.S.T. inspection to arrive aerodrome by The D.V.O. Car Expedition + inspect the H.Q. Sect. & 3rd Sect. + appears to be pleased with what he saw. The 2nd Section is still out with the Bde HQ 3rd Sect with the 5th Bde. Moor Phie 4th Sect is also now attached to Sri H.Q. te - M.T drums our return -	AH4
WAMIN	7.	Friday	Same billets - Again there in much activity - at first 1st Section remains to return with 3rd Bde -	M4
	8.	Saturday	Same billets - Usual Camp duties & found in his manner - A holiday in afternoon. L'throw sports & Concert at Reserve Park in evening -	M5
	9.	Sunday	Same billets - Usual Sunday duties. Church Parade. Sir Car officer under inspection -	M4

WAR DIARY
or
INTELLIGENCE SUMMARY

Army Form C. 2118.

2nd Can. Div. June 14, T. By. Arty.

September 1917

Place	Date	Hour	Summary of Events and Information	Remarks and references to Appendices
ETREE	10.	Monday	Same billets. Wet. Coup. drills, parades. Inspection of mules of No 1 Sect at 3 p.m. & first our own, in next few wks. Firing of some movements of B.M.G. in 3rd Fd. Bde.	
WAMIN				
"	11.	Tuesday	Same billets. Usual Camp duties, parades. Received a foot order from R.D. F&T in out. Gun. are on 2 hrs. notice. At 7 p.m. orders were received from "Q" to pack up and move to 4 Pole line at MONCHEL in the morning."	
ETREE				
WAMIN				
MONCHEL	12.	Wednesday	Same billets. Clearing up Camp & markings. Company H.Q. & 1 & 4 Sections parade at 10 a.m. moved to MONCHEL arriving at 1 p.m. Billets were taken over. No 2 Sect. which was attached to No 4 Poly. report for duty with the exception of 3 Teams with 3rd Howers. 3rd Siege are still up with 5 Poly. at VILLERS. D HOPITAL	

Army Form C. 2118.

WAR DIARY
or
INTELLIGENCE SUMMARY.

(Erase heading not required.)

Instructions regarding War Diaries and Intelligence Summaries are contained in F. S. Regs., Part II. and the Staff Manual respectively. Title pages will be prepared in manuscript.

2½ Com. Sn. Aux. H.T. Coy [?]

Place	Date	Hour	Summary of Events and Information	Remarks and references to Appendices
MONCHEL	13th	Thursday	September 1917. Section settled down in new billets at MONCHEL. Sent 17 teams to draw 4 Bn. supplies from railhead at FREVENT.	JM.
"	14th	Friday	Some billets. Sent 17 teams to draw 4 Bn. supplies from railhead at FREVENT. Remainder returning camp duties &c.	W.
"	15th	Saturday	Same billets. Sent 20 teams to draw 4 Bn. supplies. Also 7 teams to draw rations from LIGNY. Usual camp duties in &c. billets. 4 Bn. recruits [?]	W.
"	16th	Sunday	Same billets. Sent 10 teams to draw rations. &c. Usual minor fatigues. Fine day.	W.

2353 Wt. W2544/1454 700,000 5/15 D.D.&L. A.D.S.S./Forms/C. 2118.

Army Form C. 2118.

2d Corps Siege Ammn. H.T. Coy
A.S.C.

WAR DIARY
or
INTELLIGENCE SUMMARY

(Erase heading not required.)

Place	Date	Hour	Summary of Events and Information	Remarks and references to Appendices
	September 1917			
MONCHEL	17th Monday		Same billets. 20 Teams to Pratt & Woods Camp — nothing to do. Commence applying linseed oil —	
	18th Tuesday		Same billets. 20 Teams to Frevent to return to Pratt & Woods Camp — nothing to do. Five weeks.	
	19th Wednesday		Same billets. 20 Teams to Frevent to return to Pratt & Woods Camp — nothing to do. Fine weather.	JWL
	20th Thursday		Same billets. 20 Teams to Frevent to return to Pratt & Woods Camp — nothing to do.	
	21st Friday		Same billets. 20 Teams to Frevent to return to Pratt & Woods 1 Team to work.	
	22nd Saturday		Same billets. 20 Teams to Frevent to return to Pratt & Woods. 8 Teams to Govt. from S.O.S. Dete Dump.	

Army Form C. 2118.

WAR DIARY
or
INTELLIGENCE SUMMARY.

(Erase heading not required.)

2nd Can Div. Aux. H.T. Coy.

Place	Date	Hour	Summary of Events and Information	Remarks and references to Appendices
MONCHEL	23rd	Sunday	Some little. 20 Teams & Limber to clean Rations & Forage to Bde. Wind caused difficulties. Very fine weather.	nil
"	24th	Monday	Some little. do	nil
"	25th	Tuesday	Some little. do	nil
"	26th	Wednesday	Some little. Some stables & horses De. ASC. (b.b. Scott (Dick.)) arrived at 3 pm and made an inspection of the Company & stating he made lines little ideas to the separate ½ to staff & had orders to turn & issue NOT to Limits have better use. They to be several movements from Forestier of the Company this day held the De-tanks to say at AIRE railway station (95) The Canadian Labour came up by train from ARBEVILLE. Fire was created by a smokeless source in breakfast which came to lunch breeze.	nil

Army Form C. 2118.

WAR DIARY
or
INTELLIGENCE SUMMARY.
(Erase heading not required.)

2nd Coy. B.N.
Army H.T.C. B.E.F.

Place	Date	Hour	Summary of Events and Information	Remarks and references to Appendices
MONCHEL	27		September 1917	
			Thursday. Snow White. Same work as on 23rd unit section Horse Camp - Company drill.	
	28		Friday. Snow White.	
	29		Saturday. Snow White. 10 ASC Drivers sent from H.A.S.C. Train transfer to RFA Drivers. Snow White. Convoy guides from valuable.	
	30		Sunday.	

30. 9. 17.

O.C., 2nd Coy. B.N. Army H.T. Coy. B.E.F.

Vol 16

Confidential

WAR DIARY

OF

2nd East'n Div Auxiliary Horse Transport Coy R.A.S.C

FROM 1st October 1917. TO 31st October 1917.

(VOLUME N° 38.)

WAR DIARY or INTELLIGENCE SUMMARY

Army Form C. 2118.

2nd Cavalry Divisional Amn. M.T. Coy. A.S.C.

Place	Date	Hour	Summary of Events and Information	Remarks and references to Appendices
MONCHEL	October 1917			
	1st Monday		Same billets. 20 Teams daily to FREVENT Railhead to draw rations to for 4th Div. Head Quart. Train. Clothing re-fit by tailors. Staff & 10 Drivers (A.S.E) arrive to replace R.F.A Drivers - drewths	OM.
	2nd Tuesday		Same billets. Same as above but 10 extra Teams to draw weeks supply of feed from S. Clemen Dump nr FREVENT.	My
	3rd Wednesday		Same billets. Same as above (10 extra) but (10 extra) Teams to draw weeks supply feed from S. Clemen yard at LIGNY - 6 Drivers R.F.A returned to Para - wet day -	My
	4th Thursday		Same billets. O.C. Company proceeds to BACHIMONT & inspects new bivouac area. Rations to drawn from FREVENT as usual, wet day -	My
	5th Friday		Same billets. Same ration as from FREVENT as usual.	My
	6th Saturday		Same billets. Return drawn by M.T. Rumour to moving. 15 Teams drew Timber from BACHIMONT - tamps is at MONCHEL - To be drawn under D.A.D & 2nd Sup forms Ca13/14. T. & summer. Keys not taken. But all the ends full of sun under term.	My

Army Form C. 2118.

WAR DIARY
or
INTELLIGENCE SUMMARY.
(Erase heading not required.)

2nd Cav. Bde.
Army H.T. Cy. A+E

Instructions regarding War Diaries and Intelligence
Summaries are contained in F.S. Regs., Part II.
and the Staff Manual respectively. Title pages
will be prepared in manuscript.

21

Place	Date	Hour	Summary of Events and Information	Remarks and references to Appendices
	October 1917.			
MONCHEL	7th	Sunday	Saw B'dier. Sent out at team to Bde. tactics in to Bis: intent to exception to 6th coy this open animals. Practising up with him tomorrow to St Pol ans to move - one vehicle an 1 to at RAMECOURT. Distance 8 miles.	Md.
to	8th	Monday	March from Billets in MONCHEL en rout to RAMECOURT at 9 am. arrive on 11 am. Confortable billets. Morale Supply "Column" is billeted in Same Village. Rain to afternoon.	
RAMECOURT	9th	Tuesday	Remain in billets on RAMECOURT. Guns to x to Ride to St Pol in afternoon.	Md.
"	10th	Wednesday	Same billets. Exercise Greeme Horses. m dy.	
"	11th	Thursday	Same billets. do	
"	12th	Friday	Same billets. do	
"	13th	Saturday	Same billets. do	Md.

WAR DIARY
INTELLIGENCE SUMMARY

Army Form C. 2118.

3rd Cav. Bde. / 2nd Cav. Bde. / Aux. H.T.S.

Place	Date	Hour	Summary of Events and Information	Remarks and references to Appendices
RAMICOURT	October 1917. 14th Sunday		Same billets.	
"	15th Monday		Same billets. Usual work went on.	
"	16th Tuesday		Same billets. Two new horses, Mrs. S. Cann, handed to troops out return.	
"	17th Wednesday		Same billets. Mrs. S. Cann. Works up repairs etc.	
"	18th Thursday		ken in new Stall on 19th inst. Man detailed in C at Bde [?] [?] to cover — Same billets. Filling work + usual + manure.	
"	19th Friday		Cleaning up billets etc.	
RAMICOURT TO FM LEROY	20th Saturday		travelled from RAMICOURT to FM LEROY at 9am arrived 11.30am. Marched at 8.30am. HEM—FIENVILLERS—DOMART arrived in billets at 3pm	
FM LEROY TO ST LEGER	21st Sunday		O.C. Company left 6.45am on leave to England. Marched from billets at ST LEGER en route to BUYON via AMIENS attached to the 4th Brigade. Arrived in billets 5.30pm. Marched from billets from LEROY to ST LEGER via H.T. VISEE—BUYON	
ST LEGER TO BUYON			AMIENS. 4 killometres from AMIENS, heard gun fire and several aeroplane. Saw aeroplane flying high travelling in a North Easterly direction.	

Army Form C. 2118.

WAR DIARY
or
INTELLIGENCE SUMMARY.

2nd Cav Divnl
Aux HT Coy A.S.C.

(Erase heading not required.)

Instructions regarding War Diaries and Intelligence Summaries are contained in F. S. Regs., Part II. and the Staff Manual respectively. Title pages will be prepared in manuscript.

Place	Date	Hour	Summary of Events and Information	Remarks and references to Appendices
	October 1914			
BUYON	22nd Monday		Same billets. Accomodation for mules and horses in back the only available building being in bad repair.	AH3
"	23rd Tuesday		Same billets. Sent one team to Railhead SALEUX for mens rations. Raining all day. All animals under cover.	AH3
"	24th Wednesday		6 teams daily to SALEUX Railhead to draw supplies for supply Officer Div. H.Qrs - St. SAUFLIEU. Received Off detachment - 1 team from H.Qrs A.S.C. 1 team 2nd Signal Squadron and 3 teams from Divnl H.Qrs.	AH3
"	25th Thursday		Same billets. 6 teams as usual to Railhead.	AH3
"	26th Friday		Same billets. Teams as usual. Inspection of arms and equipment. Attended Court of Enquiry at H.Qrs 2nd Cav Reserve Park at BACOUEL.	AH3
"	27th Saturday		Same billets. Teams as usual to Railhead SALEUX. Weather dry + cold.	AH3
"	28th Sunday		Same billets. 5 teams to Railhead SALEUX.	AH3
"	29th Monday		Same billets. 5 teams to Railhead SALEUX.	AH3
"	30th Tuesday		Same billets. Teams to SALEUX as usual. Attended court of enquiry at H.Qrs 2nd Cav Reserve Park.	AH3
"	31st Wednesday		Same billets. Teams to SALEUX as usual. Sent team to 2nd Cavalry Divisional School, BUSSY-LES-DAOURS. 2 Reinforcements arrived from Base.	AH3

Confidential

WAR DIARY

of

2nd Cars Auxiliary (Horse) Transport Coy A.S.C

from 1st November 1917 to 30 November 1917

VOLUME N° 39

Aux HT Coy
17

Army Form C. 2118.

South of AMIENS — 2nd Cavalry Divisional
Div. H.T. Coy. ASC

WAR DIARY
or
INTELLIGENCE SUMMARY.

(Erase heading not required.)

NOVEMBER — 1917

Place	Date	Hour	Summary of Events and Information	Remarks and references to Appendices
BUYON	1st Thursday		Same billets. 2 Teams to Rail-head SALEUX for rations & Sup. Tpt.	
"	2nd Friday		5 Teams Cartel Purchase Board Bought BOVES. to draw hay - clipping -	
"			Same billets. 5 Teams to Rail-head. One additional team to 2nd Cav. Div. School at BUSSY-LES-DAOURS. Batt. proceed to DIEPPE for remounts.	
"	3rd Saturday		Same billets. 5 Teams to Rail-head to move -	
"	4th Sunday		do —	
"	5th Monday		do — receive authority 2 extra soldiers.	
"	6th Tuesday		additional to W. Establishments.	
"	7th Wednesday		do — The 11 teams attached to 3rd Cav Bde —	
"			undergone at VERS have been under orders to T.O. 3rd Cav Bde -	
"	8th Thursday		Same billets - 5 Teams to Rail-head for rations as usual -	
"	9th Friday		do —	
"	10th Saturday		do — OC. ASC came over to BUYON. Have duties re -	

WAR DIARY
or
INTELLIGENCE SUMMARY.

(Erase heading not required.)

Army Form C. 2118.

2 Cavalry Div'
Aux. 1st T. Coy.

Instructions regarding War Diaries and Intelligence Summaries are contained in F. S. Regs., Part II. and the Staff Manual respectively. Title pages will be prepared in manuscript.

Place	Date	Hour	Summary of Events and Information	Remarks and references to Appendices
BUYON	Nov 11th Sunday		Same billets. Fatigue 5 Teams forest duty in woods.	
"	12 Monday		— do — Reconns for men.	
"	13 Tuesday		— do — Reconns for new billets W & S	
"	14 Wednesday		— do — O.C. wounded from work, mostly in	
"	15 Thursday		Reserve Park. Forge + dinner from H.Q. Same billets. Issue out teams & bits or usual fair & morning. Go in to AMIENS for supplies.	
"	16 Friday		Leave BUYON at 12 noon and march to PROYART awaits orders. Elements to PROYART where we arrive at 9 p.m. Straight in 6 teams — distance 25 miles.	
PROYART	17 Saturday		Leave PROYART at 5 p.m. and march to TERTRY at 2 a.m. + several pause.	
TERTRY	18 Sunday		Company in march to at 6 p.m. All horses unfit to first team.	
TERTRY	19 Monday		Stand down. Up with Ammunition as usual 2700 13pm 4 about 460 500 S.A.A. 4c. 4c. Report completion to Q at Division. Cleaning up in afternoon.	

WAR DIARY
or
INTELLIGENCE SUMMARY.

Army Form C. 2118.

Place	Date	Hour	Summary of Events and Information	Remarks and references to Appendices
TERTRY	20th	Tuesday	November 1917. This is 2 day after we left Villiers-Faucon. During the night Cavalry moved from Tertry to area N.W. of Monchy-Lagache V.5 (central) 62.d. which is just N.W. of Monchy-Lagache. We are joined here by some of B Echelon + reinforcements under Major Welch at The Cavinium. Attack on Cambrai commenced at 6 a.m.	
MONTECOURT	21st	Wednesday	"Stew" in same billet V.5. Battle continues.	
"	22nd	Thursday	do	
"	23rd	Friday	do	
"	24th	Saturday	do	
"	25th	Sunday	Receive instructions from Q.C. to march via Quimat at Tincourt which is done in 1 day. Same as for 21st to	
"	26th	Monday	Receive order to march to Bouley near Tincourt + billet	

WAR DIARY
or
INTELLIGENCE SUMMARY.

Army Form C. 2118.

2nd Cav. Div.
Aux. H.T.C. AFO

November 1917.

Place	Date	Hour	Summary of Events and Information	Remarks and references to Appendices
MONTE- COURT-	27.	Tuesday	MONT & BOVELY known as 10 am leaving 12 men for fuel and what is news + huts - Prusher via hut + mts.	
BOVELY VIA TINCOURT.	28.	Wednesday.	Still in billets and Châtin at BOVELY - Awaiting orders. Heavy fighting continues round BOURLON Wood & Village & - Cav. Div in Trenches. Battle still going on.	
- to -	29.	Thursday	Some billets. Await Orders.	
- to -	30.	Friday.	Same billets. C. have packed in huts at GONNIEHE & GOUZEAUCOURT. Bussus are reported driven and open. Awaiting orders.	

7.12.17

Ph Russell Capt.
O.C. 2nd Cav. Div. Aux H.T.C. AFO

Vol 184

Confidential

WAR DIARY

OF

2nd Cav Div Aux H. J. Coy. R. E.

FROM 1st December 1918 TO 31st December 1918.

VOLUME N° 40.

WAR DIARY
INTELLIGENCE SUMMARY

Army Form C. 2118.

Aux. H.T. Coy. ASC

Place	Date	Hour	Summary of Events and Information	Remarks and references to Appendices
			December 1917	
BOUCLY / TINCOURT	1st	Saturday	Billeted in ruins of BOUCLY, awaiting orders - burnt of [?] have received up [?] FINS te. Heavy fighting.	
"	2nd	Sunday	Same billets. Awaiting orders. Heavy fighting.	
"	3rd	Monday	Same billets.	Hard frost.
"	4th	Tuesday	Same billets. Christian services. Town parade. Had pork.	
"	5th	Wednesday	" [?] Same billets. Then division coming back, Oak & Fred [?] fort are dumped at BOUCLY to [?]	
"	6th	Thursday	Same billets. Still no work on [?] Billets in CARTIGNY at [?] gave oats fed te 1st Div. & [?] at Team to [?] in mud.	
CARTIGNY	7th	Friday	March from CARTIGNY to DADURS distance about 30 miles in rear of Division. Arrived 9 pm - very cold. Some rain. Roads [?] in & around DADURS my bad.	WL
DADURS	8th	Saturday	March from DADURS to billets in BUYON in rear of Division. Distance about 16 miles. Some rain. Roads bad. Noticed [?] some few tanks who had my Teams a team had just new heavy boots on them. Chiefly met these [?] into to follow	WL

Army Form C. 2118.

WAR DIARY
or
INTELLIGENCE SUMMARY.

2nd Cavalry Brit.
Ass H.T. Cy. A.E.C.

(Erase heading not required.)

Instructions regarding War Diaries and Intelligence Summaries are contained in F. S. Regs., Part II. and the Staff Manual respectively. Title pages will be prepared in manuscript.

Place	Date	Hour	Summary of Events and Information	Remarks and references to Appendices
BUYON	9th Sunday		December 1917. Still down to all block at this place. Sent to clean up huts &c. With the exception of 6 1/2 men and Company H.Q. Details, all remainder are on our attaches to his 4 micro units.	nil.
"	10th Monday		Saw Block. D.A.A. + Q.M.G. (Capt Russell) Services at 11 am and instructed me to move up Forward 2 Amb. Quelch at SALEUX on arr — Arrive SALEUX 2 pm + took over new Quarters there.	
SALEUX	11th Tuesday		Settled down in new quarters — There are Forth and Sixths + to fifties. Recon down 6 pm to drive to VERS in morning.	nil
"	12th Wednesday		March to VERS and take over block from O.C. Army Relay R.H.A. We meet accommodation from 6 pm. Got settled down with	nil
VERS	13th Thursday		Cleaning up and endeavouring to improve the block —	nil
"	14th Friday		do Mutual Inspection —	nil
"	15th Saturday		do Inspection followed by O.C. —	

Army Form C. 2118.

WAR DIARY
or
INTELLIGENCE SUMMARY
(Erase heading not required.)

Place	Date	Hour	Summary of Events and Information	Remarks and references to Appendices
VERS.	16th	Sunday	December 1917. In Same Billets. Church Parade. Frosty.	
"	17th	Monday	In Same Billets. Training action re. Enemy flat forms.	
"	18th	Tuesday	do hard frost.	
"	19th	Wednesday	do	
"	20th	Thursday	do 5 Teams returned from luck	
"	21st	Friday	do 6 Teams from Stores from BOVES	
"	22nd	Saturday	do Selvis Stores to luck	
"	23rd	Sunday	do 10 Teams down Stores from BOVES	
"	24th	Monday	do previous Same.	
"	25th	Tuesday	do Xmas day. Holiday.	
"	26th	Wednesday	Company Dinner. General Leave. Officials Artistes. Same Billets.	

WAR DIARY or INTELLIGENCE SUMMARY

2 Can. Div. Amm. H.T. Coy.

Army Form C. 2118.

Place	Date	Hour	Summary of Events and Information	Remarks and references to Appendices
VIERS	27th Thursday		December 1917. Same week. Usual Company duties.	
"	28th Friday		do	
"	29th Saturday		do	
"	30th Sunday		do — Find 3 extra teams to draw rations for Brit. School which have moved to DURY — also 5 teams for wood.	W.B.
"	31st Monday		Same week — Usual Company duties — Sepultures —	
			1-1-18	

Jn Bennell Capt.
O.C.
2 Can. Div. Amm. H.T. Coy

WK 19.

Confidential

War Diary

of

2nd Cavalry Divisional Auxiliary Horse Transport Coy

from 1st January 1918 to 31st January 1918

Volume XLI

WAR DIARY or INTELLIGENCE SUMMARY

Army Form C. 2118.

2nd Cavalry Divisional Aux. H.T. Coy. A.S.C.

1316

Place	Date	Hour	Summary of Events and Information	Remarks and references to Appendices
VERS	1st Tuesday January 1916		Company H.Q. and a few teams billeted at VERS. (17 Teams in all) Chiefly employed in drawing straw wood & forage for Pack Animals. 1 Team with horses to H.Q. O.C. A.S.C. The remaining 3 Teams are on our side the river units with the horses assisting his Bgd. Transport. This number includes 3 Teams w/o Con. Echelon. Sick men and hard frost.	Jul.
"	2nd Wednesday		Same billets at VERS. Same duties. No excl. Pay Coy.	
"	3rd Thursday		do — Pan in snow W.E.	Jul.
"	4th Friday		17 Teams + 12 Teams R.P.'s do work for 5th Army – XVIII Corps. Same billets at VERS. O.C. A.S.C. arrives in afternoon and gives me much WE above 24 Teams on 6am 5th inst. C. PROYART. Latis intimation arrives from Q. enquiring exact whereabouts to start us arrival as PROYART 1st XVIII Corps for order and accommodation.	Jul.
"	5th Saturday		March to 6am there whole ft W exception 2 Farriers + 6 men + 3 sick animals. Roads very bad and slippery. Arrives at PROYART on 4.30 pm. No billets were ever awaiting. At 9.30 pm Coy was in stables & bil. OR. Luck the few men marched down to PROYART on info	Jul.

WAR DIARY
INTELLIGENCE SUMMARY

Army Form C. 2118.

2ⁿᵈ Cav. Bde. 1916
Aus. H.T. Cy. A.E.

Place	Date	Hour	Summary of Events and Information	Remarks and references to Appendices
PROYART	January 1916			
	6ᵗʰ Sunday		OC. Chapman rides on to 61ˢᵗ Divn. "Q" at HARBONNIÈRES. receive instructions to send 15 teams to 11Q & Div. at that place there and to Camp Comm! 61ˢᵗ Divn. 6 Teams are to be sent to 184ᵗʰ Bde at ROSIÈRES. This takes all my Teams and leaves me with 28 All ranks + 11 animals stranded at PROYART. Came over curved in 4 3 ton Steam hauled mot. trucks OC. A.S.C. Lorry to bring me back. Remain at PROYART with remainder from H.Q. in billet of picture return.	Nil
"	7ᵗʰ Monday		Are to have to bring me back. Same billets as before.	Nil
"	8ᵗʰ Tuesday		Lorry came at 10. am & brought back support detail - her wagon with sul kit etc. & was ordered to leave about an hour and behind in charge of a man Freeman Thorne went in town to pick it up when it returned from 61ˢᵗ Divn. (Mr Major) Battie Gore had ammunition returned to VERS & road. In my way all day the much from trench. Route via rel IN H.T. Lorry arrived VERS in 2 torn. Principals to at 9 pm.	Nil

WAR DIARY
or
INTELLIGENCE SUMMARY

Army Form C. 2118.

Place	Date	Hour	Summary of Events and Information	Remarks and references to Appendices
IERS	January 1918			
"	9. Wednesday		Settled down in all billets. No train left in Wimfour which I am in standing orders.	
"	10. Thursday		Same billets. Thin frost.	
"	11. Friday		Same billets. Expecting lorries back from 61 Division.	
"	12. Saturday		My hut keep [...] from OE.AFE to Sir E.Church. Same billets. [...]	
"	13. Sunday		Same billets. Expecting lorries back from 61. & 30 Divisions.	
"	14. Monday		Same billets. 30 lorries tier to [...] F.P.E.M.	
"	15. Tuesday		Same billets. rain.	
"	16. Wednesday		Same billets. rain.	
"	17. Thursday		Same billets. Rain now to the OE.AFE. reference to ascertaining the [...] and [...] kept by XVIII Corps.	

Army Form C. 2118.

WAR DIARY
or
INTELLIGENCE SUMMARY.

2d. Cav. Div.
Army. A.T. Cay. H.Q.

(Erase heading not required.)

Place	Date	Hour	Summary of Events and Information	Remarks and references to Appendices
VERS	January 1918			
	18th Friday		Same billets. Wire de Brebier who is now with XVIII Corps to keep me informed as to his whereabouts.	
"	19th Saturday		Same billets. Ride over to DC. HQE Army Pay. fine stay well.	
"	20th Sunday		Same billets.	
"	21st Monday		Same billets. Ride to LINEUX. 5th Bde Liaison. Inspected my teams there. Put up with S.O.	
"	22nd Tuesday		Same billets. Inspect 2 teams with R. Scots. Suspt x Visit HQ 5 Bde (?) AUBONVILLERS order them 1 Team from Brebius and 1 Team which was attached to 61st & 30th Divs from self with XVII Corps EVERS after being out once 6 mos. They were attacked by Team with Ro Humans at HORNOY and much destroyed suffering from EPIZOOTIC LYMPHANGITIS. ADVS who informs me on arrival of mine add. 20.14 had been	
"	23rd Wednesday		Same billets. Inspect 3 Teams with R. Queen & Fs. Mtd Stn in THIEULLOY and St AUBIN - Return to VERS same day.	
"	24th Thursday		Same billets. Hear we will war fever much obliteration or Epizootic Lymphangitis but this animal was isolated a few days before on fit.	
"	25th Friday			

Army Form C. 2118.

WAR DIARY
or
INTELLIGENCE SUMMARY.
(Erase heading not required.)

Instructions regarding War Diaries and Intelligence Summaries are contained in F. S. Regs., Part II. and the Staff Manual respectively. Title pages will be prepared in manuscript.

2ⁿᵈ Cav. Bri͡g A.H.T. Coy.

Place	Date	Hour	Summary of Events and Information	Remarks and references to Appendices
VERS			January 1918	
"	26	Saturday	In same billets. 6 Tenues duty in Rest Room +1 for an man return to an tht travelling Tenum.	
"	27	Sunday	do	
"	28	Monday	do — two horses to French men (officers)	
"	29	Tuesday	Frost — again at night — Same billets. Same duties — from a.m. night —	
"	30	Wednesday	Same billets — do Germ Pay Company	
"	31	Thursday	Same billets. French Armies District — Advanced Guard Coys. SAILEUX. 1 tonn Genvillin & AMIENS — returning 6.20 train on 1/2/18 for new area.	

3/1/18.

J.R. Russell Capt.
OC
2ⁿᵈ Cav. Bri͡g H.T. Cy. A.S.C.

No 20

Confidential.
War Diary
2nd Canadian Corps H.Q. Troops a.s.c.
from Feb 1 to Feb 28 1918

Volume XXXII

WAR DIARY
INTELLIGENCE SUMMARY

Army Form C. 2118.

3rd Cavalry Div.
Aus. A.T. Coy

Place	Date	Hour	Summary of Events and Information	Remarks
VERS	1st Friday		Still in billets at VERS. Cleaning up billets, clothing etc.	
"	2nd Saturday		Some billets. Packing up for march to PROYART - 15 minutes.	
" PROYART	3rd Sunday		March out of VERS at 9 am arr. PROYART 6 pm. Some evening 25 mile march, roads bad, with sleet - lorries out & with full down, roads in need at PROYART also where when injured. Bivouack in village for night.	
PROYART to MONS	4th Monday		March to MONS at 11 am train then about 4 pm distance 15 miles. Take over billets from O.C. 4 Div. A.H.T. Coy. In Sergts Rooms. "Set settled in billets" evening up to 10 Tenders arrived from the 3rd Bde.	
MONS	5th Tuesday			
"	6th Wednesday		Some billets. O.C. 4 Div. A.H.T. Coy leaves for VERS.	
"	7th Thursday		Some billets. Inspection of billets thru by O.C. Coy. Repairs noted. 7 team return from A. 13 Bde. 30" Lorries return with their 3 mule teams.	
"	8th Friday		Some billets. 1 Wagon & 2 lorries sent to R.E. Percent for enamelin in water tank. 14 Teams during return from Rail Head.	
"	9th Saturday		Some billets. Teams returned by L.S. Bde. 14 Teams during return R. Head. Mr. Wilkie employed in Div. Canten.	

Army Form C. 2118.

WAR DIARY
or
INTELLIGENCE SUMMARY.
(Erase heading not required.)

Instructions regarding War Diaries and Intelligence Summaries are contained in F. S. Regs., Part II. and the Staff Manual respectively. Title pages will be prepared in manuscript.

2nd Can. Div. Aux. H.T. Co. A.S.C.

Place	Date	Hour	Summary of Events and Information	Remarks and references to Appendices
			February 1916.	
MONS en CHAUSSÉE	10th	Sunday	Same billets. 14 Tenon Ration, R.H. 5 Tenon old dutin. Cleaning up camp etc.	
"	11th	Monday	Same billets. 22 Tenon Ration, R.H. 5 Tenon old dutin. Cleaning up camp etc.	
"	12th	Tuesday	Same billets. do 1 W.S.O. Clerk returned from leave.	
"	13th	Wednesday	184 Cpl. R.E. to go into hosp. sick to have tonsils out. Same billets. Same duties. 1 Private Road Train dutin.	
"	14th	Thursday	Same billets. Same dutin.	
"	15th	Friday	do do	
"	16th	Saturday	Very hard frost. 5 W.S.O Tanks which from R.E. Picardie. 2 air raids on same evening, 1 to Ath, 1 to VERMAND. Same billets. Same duties. No Raid here daily. They have forts.	
"	17th	Sunday	Two W.S.O Tanks sent in, we took 1 3rd + 2 Pvt. HQ. Presented to holdar whom to expr. Commander. C.S.M. P.S.M. & C.Q.M.S. before to M.S.M. Two or also too W.O Next term untill the 1st November in this Company —	
"	18th	Monday	Same billets. Church(?) cell. Same dutin —	

A5834 Wt. W4973/M687 750,000 8/16 D.D. & L. Ltd. Forms/C.2118/13.

Army Form C. 2118.

WAR DIARY
or
INTELLIGENCE SUMMARY.

2nd Cavalry Divisional A.H.T. Coy. B.E.F.

(Erase heading not required.)

Instructions regarding War Diaries and Intelligence Summaries are contained in F. S. Regs., Part II. and the Staff Manual respectively. Title pages will be prepared in manuscript.

Place	Date	Hour	Summary of Events and Information	Remarks and references to Appendices
MONS en CHAUSSEE	23rd		Saturday - February 1918 Same work - Same duties a Rail-head duty - 7/2 Brebres Run & Expend -	ML
	24th	Sun	Same work - Previously same duties daily -	ML

1.3.18.

The Russell Capt.
OC 2nd Cav. Div. A.H.T. Coy.
A.E.C.

Confidential   96 21.

War Diary

2nd Cavalry Divisional Auxiliary Horse Transport Coy

from March 1st 1918 to March 31st 1918

Volume No. XXXIII

WAR DIARY / INTELLIGENCE SUMMARY

Army Form C. 2118.

2⁴ Cavalry Bn²
Aux. H.T. Coy. R.E.

Place	Date	Hour	Summary of Events and Information	Remarks and references to Appendices
MONS en CHAUSSÉE			March 1918	
	1st Friday		In billets – checks round the Sugar Factory – 22 Tenders during	
			stations – duty from BRIE. Workshops wagon & units. Postern which	
			included one Tank Wagon attached – Cash from	
			Some billets. Some duties. First issue my coal.	
"	2nd Saturday		— do —	
"	3rd Sunday		— do —	
"	4th Monday		— do —	
"	5th Tuesday		— do —	
"	6th Wednesday		— do —	
"	7th Thursday		— do — Inspection of Rifles & Bayonets Supt. S.Laurence	
			Some return & precautions to be taken in event of retirement.	
"	8th Friday		Some billets. Some duties. Musketry Practice (no men detailed for rea-	
			-gent. Testing ammunition –	
"	9th Saturday		Some billets. Some duties. Inspection of Rifles by Cannon Supt. S.Laurence	
			Returns. Bn. turns rien – O.C. Rein. num. H.T. 12 Cav. Bn.	
"	10th Sunday		Some billets. Some duties. Cannons Supt. upon effects.	
			— do — — do — O.C. A.H.T. 12 Cav. Bn. Come rei –	
"	11th Monday		Am Commander inspects our billets. New 1st Division uncern w	
			13th inst. O.C. 3d Cav. Bn. A.H.T. Comes over to see him whilst with a	
			over a taking over on 13th inst.	

Army Form C. 2118.

WAR DIARY
or
INTELLIGENCE SUMMARY

2nd Cav. Div.
Army H.T. Coy. A.S.C.

(Erase heading not required.)

Instructions regarding War Diaries and Intelligence Summaries are contained in F. S. Regs., Part II. and the Staff Manual respectively. Title pages will be prepared in manuscript.

Place	Date	Hour	Summary of Events and Information	Remarks and references to Appendices
	March 1918			
MONS en CHAUSSÉE	12 Tuesday		Same billets re. Bgr. 9 Return march to such Rde. this met – various Sup. trucks for his trucks in turn – trucks fbn. Yorks: Trucks attend to Coy. H.Q. – packing up for trenches – evening up Whks.	
– do –	13 Wednesday		Leave Whks. at MONS en CHAUSSÉE shot on trucked via Hd. Qr. 2 Cav. Div. to H.T.E. and march at 9 am. to MAYCOURT where we arrive about 6 pm. via MATIGNY, HAM, GUISCARD. distance about 20 miles. Camp nr in BOIS de la CAVE.	
MAYCOURT	14 Thursday		Camped in BOIS de la CAVE. Settling down starting up lines re. Nati trucks sent out to work. fine front.	
"	15 Friday		Wagons & trucks utilised for work & stores. sup trucks – from nr supp. front supply.	
"	16 Saturday		Same Camp. 22 truons sent down within from our lines – front supply.	
"	17 Sunday		— do — — do — St Patricks day. Fine weather.	
"	18 Monday		Same Camp. Some activity. Numerous A.A. guns fire as is	
"	22 Friday		Fresh Aviateur – Expecting Enemy attack any moment.	
"	23 Saturday		Expecting to march in the morning. Heavy fighting.	

WAR DIARY
or
INTELLIGENCE SUMMARY.

Army Form C. 2118.

2nd Corps Sig. A.H.T. Coy A22

Place	Date	Hour	Summary of Events and Information	Remarks and references to Appendices
	March 1918.			
MAUCOURT	24th	Sunday.	Company H.Q. left MAUCOURT at 9.30 am and linked in with the R.P. via GRANDRU + PONTOISE & bivouac at CARLEPONT, but on march to BAILLY. Sent wires arriving about 11 p.m. slept in bivouac.	
BAILLY.	25th	Monday.	Remain in same bivouac and leave BAILLY at midnight 25.26 through Kings FORET d. LAIGUE cross R. AISNE River at CHISNY & up to E of COMPIEGNE	
COMPIEGNE	26th	Tuesday.	Were on through COMPIEGNE at 10 am and & in bivouac in fields west of COMPIEGNE. Divisions bivouac at night.	
"	27th	Wednesday	Leave COMPIEGNE next day at 11.30 am travelled to JONQUIERES. bivouac for night.	
JONQUIERES	28th	Thursday	Reviewed JONQUIERES refrain village in role telephone. Cables were up.	
"	29th	Friday.	Move from JONQUIERES to ERQUINVILLIERS. via ARSY + BAILLEU- arriving about 2.30 pm. waited for orders. Roads had been jammed in INIVERS ST MARTIN arriving same midnight.	
INOVERS ST MARTIN.	30th	Saturday	Marched at 8.30 am. to PLACHY, BUYON & HARDIVILLERS. TILLOY turned about 6.15 pm. Bivouacked on road.	
PLACHY BUYON.	31st	Sunday	A5834 Wt. W45..../M1687-750,000 8/16 D. D.L. & L. Ltd. Forms/C2118/13 PLACHY. BUYON.	

OC. 2nd Corps Sig. A.H.T.C.

WO 22

Confidential

War Diary

of

2nd Cavalry Divisional Auxiliary Horse Transport Coy.

From April 1st 1918 To April 30th 1918

Volume No. XLIV

Army Form C. 2118.

WAR DIARY
or
INTELLIGENCE SUMMARY.

(Erase heading not required.)

2nd Cav. Div. A.H.T. Coy. No. 22

Place	Date	Hour	Summary of Events and Information	Remarks and references to Appendices
	April 1918			
PLACHY	1st Monday		Bivouacked in Road W. of PLACHY, BUYON. Head Quarters at W/C B ENSBY and R. Employ - 6 truck approached S.R. Employ.	
"	2nd Tuesday		Much from PLACHY to RIVERY E. of AMIENS.	
RIVERY	3rd Wednesday		Bivouacked at RIVERY.	
"	4th Thursday		Bivouacked at RIVERY.	
"	5th Friday		Bivouacked at RIVERY. Received orders to march to AILLY-s-Noye, thence CLOCHIER. at 9 p.m. marched all night.	
AILLY-s-Noye CLOCHIER	6th Saturday		Bivouacked at AILLY-s-Noye thence CLOCHIER. on hard Road.	
"	7th Sunday		do	Employed 4 July
"	8th Monday		Two men H & L S. Wagon. Sick, bivouacked in AILLY. 4. Noye. Clochier - Cleaning up, men bath.	
"	9th Tuesday		do	
"	10th Wednesday		do — Orders to march at 5 pm to Rouvrel. Wagons and Animals not inspected men inspected	

at FAUCOURT. Wine at P. Eastline

Army Form C. 2118.

WAR DIARY
or
INTELLIGENCE SUMMARY.
(Erase heading not required.)

Place	Date	Hour	Summary of Events and Information	Remarks and references to Appendices
EAUCOURT	11th	Thursday	Bivouacked at EAUCOURT 4 miles from ABBEVILLE in winter wink. Fine day. Cleaning up. Trucks detailed returned to Ordnance.	
—do—	12th	Friday	Remainder to Amiens for S.O.S. Bivouacked at EAUCOURT in turn whilst above. Major Callender Cmdg Corps Res Q, arrived about 2pm with orders for all B Echelons to move up. Night in form in relation as shewn — The Divisional Petrol are left for filled in 4 Coys 6 D.R. T. O.C. Aux.H.T. to Cmdg on to present job to B Echelon 2nd Cav Bde. On arrival at destination orders were received from Cav Corps [move to VALUX. However KIV— French Cavalry having taken our billets in the meantime — B Echelon to Various in to French Cavalry billets at thouroughed in woods near VALUX — 14 2 Sqn Aux H.T. has an approx. str: of his 14.93's & life in ABBEVILLE.	
VALUX	13th	Saturday.	Arrive in above at VALUX about 2:30 am. Bivouacked in woods. Fine cool weather. OC Aux H.T. has an approx str: 15 remaining & own waters se on to destinations. Aux—fine day.	
—	14th	Sunday	Remain bivouacked at VALUX —	
—	15th	Monday	Remain bivouacked at VALUX —	

Army Form C. 2118.

WAR DIARY
or
INTELLIGENCE SUMMARY.

2nd (Can.) Div. Amm. H.T. Cy. A.S.C.

(Erase heading not required.)

Instructions regarding War Diaries and Intelligence Summaries are contained in F. S. Regs., Part II. and the Staff Manual respectively. Title pages will be prepared in manuscript.

Place	Date	Hour	Summary of Events and Information	Remarks and references to Appendices
VALUX.	16th	Sunday	On a/c of crowding in Rouen etc. 2nd Can. Div. "B" Echelon is sent back to Ponchel. – March to LE PONCHEL – "B" Echelon reached under 1st instr –	
Le PONCHEL	17th	Wednesday	"B" Echelon less Heavy Sec., R.P. & H.Q. Sup. col. A.H.T. Coy at ABBEVILLE) is ordered to march in 7.30 a.m. Proceeded via route to 9/7/18 of CREPY and merged en r' BARLINGHEM. Next day – Sup. col. H.Q. & A.H.T.C. arrive from ABBEVILLE an R. Teams, at 3 p.m. – Go into billets in LE PONCHEL. O.C. A.H.T. Coy.	
LE PONCHEL	18th Thursday		Strength (Reserve) A.H.T. Coy & other teams (Company – 2 Officers – 62 O.R. Animals – 69 + approx 12. arrived by rail ex. reserves for ABBEVILLE 2 Teams are still left behind – & Sub. remained attached to reserves for ABBEVILLE. The remainder of teams went in to LE PONCHEL. Company up. Machine gun drill re. Horse parades for exercise re. Walking Drill.	
LE PONCHEL	19th – 24th incl.			
VITZ VILLEROY	25th – 29th incl.		On 25th in accordance with instructions from Can. Corps. was ord. into billets in VITZ-VILLEROY. new h.q. R.Park. On 29th inst. moved from VITZ-VILLEROY & CREPY which was vacated by us – Wilhm in h. right –	

Army Form C. 2118.

WAR DIARY
or
INTELLIGENCE SUMMARY.   2nd Cav. Bde.
Aus. Lt.T. Coy A.S.C.

(Erase heading not required.)

Place	Date	Hour	Summary of Events and Information	Remarks and references to Appendices
	April 1916			
WITZ VILLEROY.	29.	Sunday.	March to CREPY en route to join Division – Distance 21 miles.	
CREPY.	30.	Tuesday.	March to ENQUINEGATTE approximately to join division about 19 miles.	
	6/5/16.			

J.H. Grimwade Capt.
OC. 2nd Cav. Bde. Aus. Lt.T.C.

Vol 23

Confidential
War Diary
of
2nd Cavalry Divisional Auxiliary Horse Transport Co.A.S.C.

From 1st May 1918 To. 31st May 1918.

Volume No. XLV

WAR DIARY or INTELLIGENCE SUMMARY

Army Form C. 2118.

2nd Cav. Bde. Aux. H.T. Coy

Place	Date	Hour	Summary of Events and Information	Remarks and references to Appendices
ENGUINEGATTE	May 1918.			
"	1st Wednesday		Head Quarters of Coy bivouacked in a field to W of village. Remainder of Company distributed with units. 2 Teams this at ABBEVILLE with ammunition column (?) Rain prevented much work.	
"	2nd Thursday		Some horse clearing up & painting etc.	
"	3rd Friday		do	
"	4th Saturday		do	
MONTCAUREL	5th Sunday		March at 6.30 am to new bivouack at MONTCAUREL - arrived by midday. No accumulation known in work -	
"	6th Monday		Bivouacked at MONTCAUREL - camp - mess in field -	
"	7th Tuesday		New milk field at MONTCAUREL. Camp rest @ 100/- for hire - went to firm to-day -	
"	8th Wednesday		Same bivouack. Cleaning up. Iron found -	
"	9th Thursday		do	

WAR DIARY
or
INTELLIGENCE SUMMARY

Army Form C. 2118.

2nd Can. Div.
Aux. H.T. Coy APC

(Erase heading not required.)

Place	Date	Hour	Summary of Events and Information	Remarks and references to Appendices
	May 1918			
MONTCAVREL	10:	Friday	Same Bivouack. Teams as this distributed in on 13th inst. Usual camp duties.	
"	11:	Saturday	Same Bivouack. Cleaning up & Painting - R.S. wagon from 3rd Dn H.Q. exchanged - (due in for repairs)	
"	12:	Sunday	Same Bivouack - Raining more today -	
"	13: to 18:	Monday Saturday	Same Bivouack. Fine weather. Cleaning up & painting re. &	
"	19:	Sunday	Same Bivouack. Same work. Village service held during the night. Usual duties re.	
"	20: 21: 22: 23:	Monday Tuesday Wednesday Thursday	Same Bivouack re. 4 Teams sent to MANINGHEM on flying carts. These were at work some days in unloading Raining all day - Same Bivouack.	
"	24:	Friday	Same Bivouack. 4 Teams again sent to MANINGHEM for	
"	25:	Saturday	Same Bivouack. 4 Teams sent duty for 4 or 5 days.	

Army Form C. 2118.

2nd Can. Div.
Army H.T. Coy

WAR DIARY
or
INTELLIGENCE SUMMARY
(Erase heading not required.)

Place	Date	Hour	Summary of Events and Information	Remarks and references to Appendices
MONTEAUREL	26	Sunday	Same bivouack	
	27	Monday	Same bivouack. Painting wagons etc usual duties. OC Company left 6 p.m. on one months leave to England	
	28	Tuesday	Same bivouack. 3 G.S. wagons teams from 3rd Bde, 3 from 4th Bde and 4 from 5th Bde sent in for overhauling and inspection. Two teams from the 5th Bde under Working Instruction for Epsoms Lymphangitis were inspected and hauled and returned this evening	
	29	Wednesday	Same bivouacks. Painting & repairing wagons etc. Horse Parade Sent 1 G.S. wagon to 5th Machine Gun Squadron while their wagon is being repaired	
	30	Thursday	Same bivouacks. Repairing harness, painting wagons etc	
	31	Friday	Same bivouacks. Repairing & Painting wagons, cleaning up etc	

J.M. Bremner 2nd Lieut
OC 2nd Can Div Aux H Toy Coy

Vol 24

Confidential

War Diary

of

2nd Cavalry Divisional Auxiliary Horse Transport Coy.

from June 1st 1918 to June 30th 1918

Volume No. XLVI

Army Form C. 2118.

WAR DIARY
or
INTELLIGENCE SUMMARY. 2ND Cav. A.H.T. Coy. A.S.C.

(Erase heading not required.)

June 1918

Place	Date	Hour	Summary of Events and Information	Remarks and references to Appendices
MONTCAVREL	June 1st Saturday		Bivouacked in a field. Usual duties. Painting and repairing wagons etc	
	2nd Sunday		Same bivouack	
	3rd Monday		Same bivouack. Inspected wagons & teams sent in from the Bdes for overhauling and returned them. 9 more wagons & teams, 3 from 3rd Cav Bde, 4 from 4th Cav Bde & 2 from 5th Cav Bde were sent in for repairs & inspection in afternoon.	
	4th Thursday		Same bivouack. Training mules. Painting wagons & repairing	
	5th Wednesday		Same bivouack. Horse Parade. Cleaning up. Repairs & painting	
	6th Thursday		Same bivouack. Painting & repairing wagons. 4 teams attached to R.A.F. at MENINGHAM returned this afternoon	
	7th Friday		Same bivouack. Usual duties, repairing & painting wagons	
	8th Saturday		Same bivouack. Usual duties. Bathing Parade. Overhauling wagons	
	9th Sunday		Same bivouack. Usual duties	
	10th Monday		Same bivouack. 9 teams sent in for repairs inspected by O.C.B.S.C. and returned. Received 7 more for overhauling	

Army Form C. 2118.

WAR DIARY
or
INTELLIGENCE SUMMARY.

(Erase heading not required.)

June 1915

Instructions regarding War Diaries and Intelligence Summaries are contained in F. S. Regs., Part II. and the Staff Manual respectively. Title pages will be prepared in manuscript.

Place	Date	Hour	Summary of Events and Information	Remarks and references to Appendices
MONTCAVREL				
June	11th Tuesday		Same bivouack. Repairing and painting wagons etc	
"	12" Wednesday		Same bivouack. Stove Parade repairing & painting wagons	
"	13" Thursday		Same bivouack. Usual duties repairing & cleaning up	
"	14" Friday		Same bivouack. Arms inspection usual camp duties Painting	
"	15" Saturday		Same bivouack. Inspected all bivouacks & tents. Painting	JKB
"	16" Sunday		Same bivouack. Inspection of harness etc	
"	17" Monday		Same bivouack. All animals wagons and harness inspected by A.D.of S&T. The 4 teams sent in from 3, 4 & 5 Can Brigades for one hauling returned after inspection	
"	18" Tuesday		Same bivouack. Usual camp duties	
"	19" Wednesday		Same bivouack. Raining all last night. Painting wagons etc	
"	20" Thursday		Same bivouack. Horse Parade Usual duties	

Army Form C. 2118.

WAR DIARY
or
INTELLIGENCE SUMMARY

(Erase heading not required.)

June 1918

Place	Date	Hour	Summary of Events and Information	Remarks and references to Appendices
MONTCAVREL	June 21st Friday		Same bivouack Cleaning up Usual duties	
	22nd Saturday		Same bivouack Usual duties	
	23rd Sunday		Same bivouack Usual duties	
	24th Monday		Same bivouack Usual duties Replaced 2 mules at 3rd Cav Bde H.Qrs	
	25th Tuesday		Same bivouack Usual duties Painting & repairing wagons	
	26th Wednesday		Same bivouack Horse Parade	
	27th Thursday		Same bivouack Usual duties Painting & repairing wagons	
	28th Friday		Same bivouack Usual duties Cashing Parade 3 miles East	
	29th Saturday		Same bivouack Usual duties Painting & cleaning up	
	30th Sunday		Same bivouack Usual duties	

J.M.Breloner 2nd Lieut
O.C. 2nd Cav Div Aux J.T Coy A.S.C

No 23

Confidential

War Diary

of

2nd Cavalry Divisional Auxiliary Horse Transport Coy A.S.C

From 1st July 1918 to 31 July 1918

Volume XLVII

Army Form C. 2118.

WAR DIARY
or
INTELLIGENCE SUMMARY

(Erase heading not required.)

2nd Cavalry Div'l Aux. Horse T. Coy

July 1918

Place	Date	Hour	Summary of Events and Information	Remarks and references to Appendices
MONTCAVREL	1st Monday		Same bivouack. Usual duties. Painting etc. Names Inspection	A&B
"	2nd Tuesday		Same bivouack. Usual duties. 2 teams for duty with 6" D 4s	A&B
"	3rd Wednesday		Same bivouack. Usual duties. 22 NCOs & men isolated and in hospital with P.U.O. 2 teams for duty with 6D 4s	A&B
"	4th Thursday		Same bivouack. Usual duties 2 teams for duty with 6D 4s	A&B
"	5th Friday		Same bivouack. Usual duties 14 NCOs & men in hospital 12 NCOs & men isolated with P.U.O. 2 teams for duty with 6D 4s. O.C. Company returned from England this afternoon.	A&B
"	6th Saturday		Same bivouack - Usual duties. 21 N.C.Os & men down with P.U.O. Same bivouack.	A&B
"	7th Sunday		do	
"	8th Monday		24 N.C.Os & men sick. P.U.O	
"	9th Tuesday		do	
"	10th Wednesday		do	

Army Form C. 2118.

WAR DIARY
or
INTELLIGENCE SUMMARY.

(Erase heading not required.)

2nd Corps, 15th Aux. H.T. Coy.

Place	Date	Hour	Summary of Events and Information	Remarks and references to Appendices
MONTCAVREL	July 1916			
	11th	Thursday	Arrived from Montreuil to BREXENT & attached to 3rd Corps Aux to assist in drawing rations by horse transport from ETAPLES.	
BREXENT	12th	Friday	On billets at BREXENT drawing up 6 P.U.O. men whilst on duty.	
"	13th	Saturday	ETAPLES to 3.15 and drove him to New Sufflin from return to duty -	5 teams
"	14th	Sunday	In billets at BREXENT. 6 P.U.O. men at TUBERSENT. Received orders early 3 am to march at 9 am and to be on standing train NEUVILLE at 10.15 am. Five horse to march to run from A.E. to new billet at WAIL distance about 24 miles.	
WAIL	15th	Monday	Leave billets at WAIL at 2.30 pm and march to new men at BERLENCOURT where we arrive about 7.30pm up at WAIL -	
BERLENCOURT	16th	Tuesday	Billets in N.End of BERLENCOURT. Drawing up - All P.U.O. hand returned to duty with the exception of 4 -	

Army Form C. 2118.

WAR DIARY
or
INTELLIGENCE SUMMARY
(Erase heading not required.)

2nd (County of London) Aux. Horse Transport Coy ASC

Place	Date	Hour	Summary of Events and Information	Remarks and references to Appendices
BERLENCOURT	17		Wednesday. Saw Killick. Studd/Ln. P.H.R. and 2 others. 11 Teams. 11 recruits are attached for work to be taken into the Division. Saw men to H.T. from M.S. F.O.11 at LE COUROY	
"	18		Thursday	
"	19		Friday. Saw Wulf. Saw Studd. Cleaning up & fitting	
"	20		Saturday. a good week - from our new F.V.O. altered lorry 3	
"	21		Sunday	
"	22		Monday. Any ration wanted 1-10 km sum. Marched to WAIL area and billeted there for the night with his Division in any - (Billets in GALAMETZ) 1/2 miles.	
WAIL	23		Tuesday - Marched to MONTCAVREL and took one Killick at his château ALETTE. distance about 24 miles - Very wet day - Arrived at	
ALETTE	24		Wednesday in billets at ALETTE. Cleaning up. about 6.15 pm -	
"	25		Thursday do do 4 horse remounts arrived	
"	26		Friday " do do by Motor arrived 1.9 km -	

Army Form C. 2118.

WAR DIARY
or
INTELLIGENCE SUMMARY.

2nd Cavalry Divl.
Aux. H.T. Coy.

(Erase heading not required.)

Place	Date	Hour	Summary of Events and Information	Remarks and references to Appendices
ALETTE	27th	Saturday	In same billets: Very wet day. Standing to and	
"	28th	Sunday	do	
			reminders out with various units in Sector.	
"	29th	Monday	In same billets - Ordinary Company duties - Horse Inspection	
"	30th	Tuesday	by actions moved 1.9 am.	
"	31st	Wednesday	do	

1/8/18.

A. Purcell
Capt.
OC
2 Cav. Div. Aux. H.T. Coy. ACC.

Confidential

War Diary

2nd Cavalry Divisional Auxiliary Horse Transport Coy.

From August 1st 1918 to August 31 1918

Volume No XLVIII

WAR DIARY / INTELLIGENCE SUMMARY

Army Form C. 2118.

2nd Can. Div. Aux. H.T. Coy. A.S.C.

AUGUST 1918.

Place	Date	Hour	Summary of Events and Information	Remarks and references to Appendices
ALETTE	1st Thursday		Bivouacked + full in billets. Have truck 6, A.O.V.s who are satisfied with Canadian personals. 10 teams in Company H.Q. remainder detailed to assist in the Divison.	
"	2nd Friday		Same billets re usual duties.	
"	3rd Saturday		Same billets – usual.	
"	4th Sunday		Same billets – Broken up have to move – lunch at 9 p.m. from Same billets broken up to move – lunch at 9 p.m. from ALETTE to REPECY via DOMPIERRE and Dinner.	
REPECY	5th Monday		Remain at REPECY all day and march to CADOURS + arrive at 4:30 a.m.	
CADOURS	6th Tuesday		Remain in CADOURS all day and march to BUIGNEY at 8:30 p.m. via suin from Piequigny	
BUIGNEY	7th Wednesday		Stand return all day on the Somme. Lorries (after ammunition) all night to 6-7 lines. Slow return from 7 am to 9 pm. About from ammunition refilled at BUIGNEY and immediately dispatch to fill up with ammunition – 75 Tons. This is completed by 11 pm. Remainder trips Artillery up – ready to march at 4 am. Printed	

WAR DIARY
INTELLIGENCE SUMMARY

Army Form C. 2118.

2nd Cavalry Divisional
Amm. S.T. Coy, ASC

Place	Date	Hour	Summary of Events and Information	Remarks and references to Appendices
	AUGUST. 1918			
BUIGNY	8th Thursday		Never from BUIGNY at 8:30 am. to BREUILLE but further to Renault Park more to 1/2 a mile to W. outskirts of MONTIÈRES. Park left main road — The 3rd Heavy Section of C.E. Pards. joined us on our way up — Total 45 O.R + 46 Horses — The following is ammunition re. carried on Company wagons. "N"(Stokes) 13 P. (H.E.) 1784 rounds — N.X.(H.E.I5 P. Q.F.) 736 Rounds, S.A.A. 514,000 rounds — Bombs. 1800 — Bennet Flare Red. 1344 " —	
MONTIÈRES	9th Friday		Company + Heavy Section field Cmd: — Bivouacked N of the main road. — W. END of MONTIÈRES —	
"	10th Saturday		do — awaiting orders —	
"	11th Sunday		do —	
"	12th Monday		do —	
"	13th Tuesday		do —	
"	14th Wednesday		do —	

Army Form C. 2118.

WAR DIARY
or
INTELLIGENCE SUMMARY.

2nd Cav Bde.
Aux H.T. Coy RHA

(Erase heading not required.)

Instructions regarding War Diaries and Intelligence Summaries are contained in F. S. Regs., Part II. and the Staff Manual respectively. Title pages will be prepared in manuscript.

Place	Date	Hour	Summary of Events and Information	Remarks and references to Appendices
	August 1918			
MONTIÈRES	15th Thursday		March to BELLOY at 4 pm from MONTIÈRES. Men to tea supper.	
BELLOY	16th Friday		March to CANAPLES. travel 4 am Men & Horses bivouack for night.	
CANAPLES	17th Saturday		March to CAUMONT leaving Aux to Crntn. Horses & am 8t distance 16 miles.	
CAUMONT	18th Sunday		Remain bivouacked. Send 1 hrs gp to OC. 3rd Pres R.H.A.	
"	19th Monday		do - - Band on reveneily freveneer & M.T. -	
"	20th Tuesday		do - do -	
"	21st Wednesday		do - - Send one Team to S.O. & Bde, & 4 Team	
"	22nd Thursday		L. O. C. R.A. return to be ready to march to night. Leave CAUMONT at 9.30 am and march on to 18th to Inf. DOULLENS & GRENAS distance about 28 miles that much — arrive at about 6 am. Bivouack with H.Q. 2 Bdium Bn Trumps (Hq & Ork)	
GRENAS	23rd Friday		Leave GRENAS about 6 pm truvel to BAILLEUMONT. arrive at 11 pm taking rations to dv. Trumps –	
BAILLEUMONT	24th Saturday		Remain bivouacked at BAILLEUMONT.	

Army Form C. 2118.

WAR DIARY
or
INTELLIGENCE SUMMARY 2nd Cav. Bri.
(Erase heading not required.) Aux. H.T. Coy A.S.C.

Instructions regarding War Diaries and Intelligence
Summaries are contained in F. S. Regs., Part II.
and the Staff Manual respectively. Title pages
will be prepared in manuscript.

Place	Date	Hour	Summary of Events and Information	Remarks and references to Appendices
BAILLEUMONT	25	Sunday	August 1916 — Leave bivouack at BAILLEUMONT and return to GRENAS arriving there above 1 pm. Send our following wagons teams to work:— 1/ Louvein. 4. — R. Scots Guys. 4 — 6 DG's 4 — Q.O.Oxfords 4 — 20 Huns 3 :— The cyclist team & horses returns to their attached to his various divisions of 3rd Army. —	
GRENAS	26	Monday	Remain in billets at GRENAS. Very wet night — 25/26 — 6 T.E. RE. Section. — Send our 1 wagon & team to 25 Huns	
"	27	Tuesday	Some Bivouack at GRENAS — Some transport as above —	
"	28	Wednesday	do — Cleaning up &c —	
"	29	Thursday	do —	
"	30	Friday	do —	
"	31	Saturday	do —	

1.9.16.

[signature] Capt.
O.C. 2nd Cav. Bri. Aux. H.T. Coy A.S.C.

No. 27.

Confidential

War Diary

of

2nd Cavalry Divisional Auxiliary Horse Transport Company.

From 1st September 1918 to 30th September 1918

Volume No. XLIX

Army Form C. 2118.

WAR DIARY
or
INTELLIGENCE SUMMARY.

(Erase heading not required.)

2nd Cavalry Divisional Aus. H.T. Coy. A.S.C.

Place	Date	Hour	Summary of Events and Information	Remarks and references to Appendices
GREVAS.	1st	Sunday	H.Q. of Company barracked in field in Grevas. Remainder of Company attached in various Brigades & Regiments for duty.	
"	2nd	Monday	do	
"	3rd	Tuesday	do	
"	4th	Wednesday	do	
"	5th	Thursday	do	
"	6th	Friday	do. They return nightly & returned to billets.	
			On Orders will all be en troops belonging to 4th Army will Red Royals, Linden Forests & ALBERT area & his Red and Green with Staff only. Take one Garden billets a/c.	
"	7th	Saturday	Same barracks at GRENAS.	
"	8th	Sunday	do	
"	9th	Monday	do	
"	10th	Tuesday	do. To are to GUERRIEU & mid out with 5 Bde who moved him on Sunday. Sir Br Barker & town and transport N McKichie & riding him.	
"	11th	Wednesday	Same barracks at GRENAS. McKichie goes on to the charge of his own brigade. Transport attached 5 Bde.	

Army Form C. 2118.

2º Cav. Bde.
Aux. 14. T. Bug A.L.C.

WAR DIARY
or
INTELLIGENCE SUMMARY.
(Erase heading not required.)

Instructions regarding War Diaries and Intelligence Summaries are contained in F. S. Regs., Part II. and the Staff Manual respectively. Title pages will be prepared in manuscript.

Place	Date	Hour	Summary of Events and Information ~ SEPTEMBER 1916 ~	Remarks and references to Appendices
GRENAS	12.	Thursday	Same bivouack - much rain - 2 Lt Birkin gone on leave.	
"	13.	Friday	Same bivouack. Raining off a times in fits in torrents.	
"	14.	Saturday	do	
"	15.	Sunday	do -- In friends have been relieved by 2 Shackle which	
"	16.	Monday	& Company H.Q. -- from 5 Bde.	
"	17.	Tuesday	Same Bivouack - rain thunder & rain - Ray day -	
"	18.	Wednesday	do --	
"	19.	Thursday	do -- Took fatigue out to Dec? with 5 Bde.	
"	20.	Friday	do -- Went to GUADIEMPRE & inspected new billets use found	
"	21.	Saturday	whiting bivouack. Rain. Cold ground.	
"	22.	Sunday	same bivouack. Cold & rain.	do
"	23.	Monday	do -- Cold turned wine --	

Army Form C. 2118.

WAR DIARY
or
INTELLIGENCE SUMMARY.

2nd Cavalry Divisional
Aux. H.T. Coy. A.S.C.

(Erase heading not required.)

Place	Date	Hour	Summary of Events and Information	Remarks and references to Appendices
GRENAS	24th September 1918	Tuesday	Same billets. 39 Teams still away with Brigades & reserve lorries. 6 Teams only left with Coy. H.Q. - 2 boys under orders away on leave - 35 in all. Some P.B. men attached to Coy. Much rain.	
"	26th	Wednesday	do - Mr. Kriecke - från one 1st C.Res. at ROISEL on 27th inst	
"	26th	Thursday	do -	
"	27th	Friday	do -	
"	28th	Saturday	do -	
"	29th	Sunday	do - 2 Lt Paterson return to leave from England	
"	30th	Monday	do - 2 Lt Paterson re-joins 5th Res. at ROISEL	

1.10.18

[signature]
OC 2nd Cav. Div. Aux. H.T. Coy. A.S.C.

13   Vol 28.

Confidential

War Diary

of

2nd Canadian Divisional Auxiliary Horse Transport Coy

From 1st October 1918 to 31st October 1918

Volume No. I

Army Form C. 2118.

WAR DIARY
or
INTELLIGENCE SUMMARY.
(Erase heading not required.)

2nd Cavalry Divisional
Amm. H.T. Co., ASC.

Place	Date	Hour	Summary of Events and Information	Remarks and references to Appendices
GRENAS	October 1918			
"	1st Tuesday		Same bivouack at Grenas — H.Q. of Company with 5 wagons. AH.T.5	
"	2nd Wednesday		remainder on with Brigades &c. Same bivouack. Ordinary Company duties —	
"	3rd Thursday		do — 1 m. kitchen orderlies from 6th Bde.	
"	4th Friday		do —	
"	5th Saturday		do — 1 m. kitchen attached to troops —	
"	6th Sunday		do —	
"	7th Monday		do — three punde.	
"	8th Tuesday		do —	
"	9th Wednesday		do —	
"	10th Thursday		do — Harness Inspection & Extras —	
"	11th Friday		do —	
"	12th Saturday		do — 3 of the Company horses transfered to Div. H.Q. Ordinary exercise from 12 Noon to 9 Hours —	

Army Form C. 2118.

2nd Cavalry Bde
Aux. M.T. Co. ACC

WAR DIARY
or
INTELLIGENCE SUMMARY
(Erase heading not required.)

Instructions regarding War Diaries and Intelligence Summaries are contained in F. S. Regs., Part II. and the Staff Manual respectively. Title pages will be prepared in manuscript.

(2)

Place	Date	Hour	Summary of Events and Information	Remarks and references to Appendices
ARRAS	Oct 13th 1918		Sunday – Same billets re. Same distribution – No 5 teams with 1st Q.F.C. and 40 teams on with various units the Division –	
"	14th		Monday – Same bivouack –	
"	15th		Tuesday – do —	
"	16th		Wednesday – Same bivouack – A.D.V.S. inspect H.Q. animals – he Kickie Serah? from Hope –	
"	17th		Thursday – Same bivouack. Setting up wet and windy. Recon. Renum. from H.Q. & were H.Q. of Canadian LRAS. Ride over to Pos and got billets – from Town Major – ZILLE Captured – 8 ½ Corps –	
"	18th		Friday – Leave Bivvies and march to PAS – arriving 11. a.m.	
PAS.	19th		Saturday – Billets on No 109 APS. and Paul Enfumable – cleaning up to	
"	20th		Sunday – Same billets as Pas. Renum –	
"	21st		Monday – do —	
"	22nd		Tuesday – do —	
"	23rd		Wednesday – do —	
"	24th		Thursday – Horse funeral.	

WAR DIARY
or
INTELLIGENCE SUMMARY.

Army Form C. 2118.

Place	Date	Hour	Summary of Events and Information	Remarks and references to Appendices
PKS			October 1918	
	25	Friday	Same billets as PAS. Company with exception to 15 known at Kirra	
	26	Saturday	this an with rout. Le Cpl. Knight on leave, kirked 4 2 muls. Same billets.	
	27	Sunday	Same billets.	
	28	Monday	Same billets.	
	29	Tuesday	Same billets.	
	30	Wednesday	Same billets. horse parade.	
	31	Thursday	Same billets. horse parade.	

T.M.G.

O.C.
2nd Can Divn. Aux. H.T. Co. A.I.F.

WO 29

Confidential

War

Diary

of

2nd Cavalry Divisional Auxiliary Horse Transport Coy A.S.C.

From November 1st 1918 to November 30. 1918

Volume No. LI

WAR DIARY

INTELLIGENCE SUMMARY

Army Form C. 2118.

2nd (Cavalry Divisional) Aux. A.T. Coy. A.S.C.

Instructions regarding War Diaries and Intelligence Summaries are contained in F.S. Regs., Part II and the Staff Manual respectively. Title pages will be prepared in manuscript.

(Erase heading not required.)

Place	Date	Hour	Summary of Events and Information	Remarks and references to Appendices
			NOVEMBER 1918	
PAS.	1st	Friday	Still billeted in PAS. Ordinary routine duties. Coy. H.Q. consists of 5 Tenners plus spare with 40 lorries and teams on site in divisional with Lt. receiving with Divisional Inspection.	
"	2nd	Saturday	Same billet. Gun convoy leaving 1 pm in.	
"	3rd	Sunday	Same billet.	
"	4th	Monday	Same billet. Gun on to LA CATELET and inspected diving him.	
"	5th	Tuesday	at 5 pm. Been Big H.Q. we join [?] convoy as backup. Packing up to move to unknown.	
"	6th	Wednesday	Same billet. Moved to ACHIET-LE-GRAND billet at	
BIHUCOURT.			BIHUCOURT.	
CAMBRAI	7th	Thursday	Moved from BIHUCOURT to CAMBRAI and station	
"	8th	Friday	in Cavalry Bks there.	
"			CAMBRAI - unknown	
BOUSIES	13th	Wednesday	Moved from Cambrai to BOUSIES	
"	14th	Thursday	Moved from BOUSIES to TASMERES	
TASMERES	15th	Friday	Moved from TASMERES to DOUZIES	
DOUZIES	16	Saturday	[?] Moved to DOUZIES [?] MAUBEUGE	

Army Form C. 2118.

WAR DIARY
or
INTELLIGENCE SUMMARY.
(Erase heading not required.)

2nd Cav. Div.
Aug. & C. G. [illegible]

MARCH nr. BELGIUM   Summary [illegible] River & Runner

Place	Date	Hour	Summary of Events and Information	Remarks and references to Appendices
MAUBEUGE	17	Sunday	Paraded 6 a.m. and moved into Jemmin & THUIN —	
			All wagons expecting 5 GSW are with LOBBES.	
THUIN	18	Monday	Moved from THUIN to HANZINELLE. The GSW is now	
			attached to 4th Army — Aft to remain here for 2 days	
MORIALME	19	Tuesday	Moved from Ruines to MORIALME.	
LOBBES				
	20	Wednesday	Moved from MORIALME to DINANT.	
	21	Thursday	Moved from DINANT to LIGNON.	
	22	Friday	Moved from LIGNON to MARCHE billets at WAHA —	
	23	Saturday	WAHA.	
	24	Sunday	WAHA.	
	25	MONDAY	WAHA.	
	26	Tuesday	WAHA. Fine train [illegible] citizens came through —	
	27	Wednesday	WAHA —	

Army Form C. 2118.

WAR DIARY
INTELLIGENCE SUMMARY.
(Erase heading not required.)

Aux. H.T. Cy. A.S.C.

Place	Date	Hour	Summary of Events and Information	Remarks and references to Appendices
NAHA. BELGIUM	28	Thursday.	Arriving Carpenter &c.	
	29	Friday.	Arriving on duties eg. 7 Cpl. S.M. Pike transferred to 13 Div. Train	
	30	Saturday.	Arriving on duties. 7/a. Q.M.S. Newton taken on duties as 7 C.S.M.	

30.XI.16.

J. Russell Capt
o.c.
v/Cav. Div. A.H.T. Cy A.S.C.

Confidential

War Diary
of
2nd Cavalry Divisional Aux. H.T. Coy. R.A.S.C.

From 1st December to 31 December 1918

Volume No. LII

Army Form C. 2118.

Inf. Div.
Aux. H.T. Coy A.S.C.

WAR DIARY
or
INTELLIGENCE SUMMARY.
(Erase heading not required.)

Place	Date	Hour	Summary of Events and Information	Remarks and references to Appendices
			December 1918	
WAHA	1. Sunday		Same billets in own work. Evel - Orderly duties	
	2.			
	5. Friday		Same billets. 41 Teams out as usual with limber	
	6. Saturday			
	7. Sunday		Same billets. Usual private employment.	
	9. Monday			
	10. Tuesday		Same billets. Do. Return to vans from 1st Cav. Bde.	
	11. Wednesday		do. at W.T.M.A.	
	12. Thursday		do. Certain parades. Div H.Q. in afternoon	
	13. Friday		Same billets. Usual duties Raining	
	14. Saturday		" C.O. left - on leave to England	
	15. Sunday		" Usual duties Inspected all animals	
VIEUXVILLE	16. Monday		H.Qrs of Company marched at 08-00 to VIEUXVILLE arriving 13.30. Rained all day	
MONT	17. Tuesday		marched at 08.00 to MONT arrived 14.30	

Army Form C. 2118.

WAR DIARY
or
INTELLIGENCE SUMMARY.

(Erase heading not required.)

2nd Cav Div
Army 1st T Coy/ ASC

Place	Date	Hour	Summary of Events and Information	Remarks and references to Appendices
MONT	December 1918			
	18th Wednesday		Billeted in MONT all animals under cover	JHB
"	19th Thursday		Same billets As a Labour Company well suitably were in line expect to be ordered to move	JHB
"	20th Friday		Same billets Inspected adjoining village JEVOUMONT and SPIXHE in case of a move found no accommodation	JHB
"	21st Saturday		Same billets One horse sent in from 5th Cav Bde	JHB
"	22nd Sunday		Same billets	JHB
"	23rd Monday		Same billets 4 mules for casting sent to 7th MV Section sent out to units for 2 Coal miners	JHB
"	24th Tuesday		Same billets Usual duties. 2 Coal miners sent to concentration camp at SERAING	JHB
"	25th Wednesday		Same billets Christmas Day. Snowing Sent 7 more coal miners to SERAING	JHB
"	26th Thursday		Same billets Raining exchanged wagon sent in from 5th Cav Bde for repairs	JHB

WAR DIARY or **INTELLIGENCE SUMMARY.**

Army Form C. 2118.

2nd Cav Div
Aux H T Coy. R A S C

Place	Date	Hour	Summary of Events and Information	Remarks and references to Appendices
MONT	27th Friday	Same billets	Usual duties. Shortage of men due to release of Coal miners	AH3
" "	28th Saturday	Same billets	Usual duties	AH3
" "	29th Sunday	Same billets	Usual duties	AH3
" "	30th Monday	Same billets	usual duties. 1 team sent in from Div H Qrs	AH3
" "	31st Tuesday	Same billets	usual duties. 2 teams sent in from 2nd Sig Squadron, 2nd Field Squadron	AH3

J H Bretmer 2" Lieut.
O.C. 2nd Cav Div Aux HT Coy RASC

Confidential

War Diary of

2nd Cavalry Divisional Auxiliary Horse Transport Coy

From 1st January 1919 To. 31st January 1919

Volume (LIII)

WAR DIARY

Army Form C. 2118.

2nd Cav Divnl
Aux H T Coy R.A.S.C.

INTELLIGENCE SUMMARY

Place	Date	Hour	Summary of Events and Information	Remarks and references to Appendices
MONT	January 1919			
	Wednesday 1st		Same billets Usual duties.	JWB
"	Thursday 2nd		Same billets. Sent AFZ16 to all men on detachment	JWB
"	Friday 3rd		Same billets Usual duties & inspections	JWB
"	Saturday 4th		Same billets Usual duties Raining Repairing wagons	JWB
"	Sunday 5th		Same billets Usual duties Raining Repairing wagons	JWB
"	Monday 6th		Same billets Collected abandoned German H T wagon Usual duties	JWB
"	Tuesday 7th		Same billets Inspected all horses usual duties	JWB
"	Wednesday 8th		Same billets C.O. granted extension of leave on medical grounds on 1-1-19 Two wagons sent to PRAYON to load German machine guns returned empty, Belgian authorities refuse to hand over	JWB
"	Thursday 9th		Same billets Usual duties Changed mule sent in from 5"Bde	JWB

Army Form C. 2118.

WAR DIARY

INTELLIGENCE SUMMARY.

(Erase heading not required.)

2nd Cav. Divnl.
Aux H.T. Coy. RASC

Place	Date	Hour	Summary of Events and Information	Remarks and references to Appendices
MIONT	Friday 10th		January 1919. Same billets. 2 teams sent to Pepinster to draw coal for Divisional troops. 1 team to PRAYON to load German machine Guns	JWB
"	Saturday 11th		Same billets. Usual inspections and duties	JWB
"	Sunday 12th		Same billets. Usual duties	JWB
"	Monday 13th		Same billets. Usual duties. Repairing wagons	JWB
"	Tuesday 14th		Same billets. Usual duties etc	JWB
"	Wednesday 15th		Same billets. Usual duties etc	JWB
"	Thursday 16th		Same billets. Usual duties etc	JWB
"	Friday 17th		Same billets. Usual duties etc	JWB
"	Saturday 18th		Same billets. Usual duties etc	JWB

Army Form C. 2118.

2nd Cav Divnl
Aux H.T. Coy R A S C

WAR DIARY
INTELLIGENCE SUMMARY.
(Erase heading not required.)

Instructions regarding War Diaries and Intelligence Summaries are contained in F. S. Regs., Part II. and the Staff Manual respectively. Title pages will be prepared in manuscript.

Place	Date	Hour	Summary of Events and Information	Remarks and references to Appendicies
MDINT	January 1919			
"	Sunday 19th		Same billets one man for demobilization sent to Concentration Camp at CONCENT	1/15
"	Monday 20th		Same billets usual duties	1/15
"	Tuesday 21st		Same billets usual duties	1/15
"	Wednesday 22		Same billets usual duties	1/15
"	Thursday 23		Same billets usual duties	1/15
"	Friday 24		Same billets usual duties	1/15
"	Saturday 25th		Same billets usual duties Snowing	1/15
"	Sunday 26		Same billets sent another man for demobilization to concentration camp(?) at CONCENT wagon and team sent in from 3rd Ferrers	1/15

WAR DIARY
INTELLIGENCE SUMMARY.
(Erase heading not required.)

Army Form C. 2118.

2nd Cav Divn
Aux: H.S. A.Q.S.

Place	Date	Hour	Summary of Events and Information	Remarks and references to Appendices
MONT	Monday 27 January 1919		Usual duties	AHS
"	Tuesday 28		Usual duties	AHS
"	Wednesday 29		Usual duties	AHS
"	Thursday 30		Same billets. Usual duties. Sent a party to Étinehem to obtain 6 carrel apparatus. Quinity given AHS	AHS
"	Friday 31		Same billets. Usual duties. All animals approved and classified by ADVS	AHS

N Brebner Lieuty
OC 2 Cav Divn Aux H.Trp Resc

Vol 32

Confidential

War Diary

of

2nd Cavalry Divisional Auxiliary Horse Transport Company

From 1st February 1919 to 28th February 1919

(Volume LIV.)

Army Form C. 2118.

WAR DIARY
or
INTELLIGENCE SUMMARY

2nd Cav Divnl
Aux H T Coy R A S C

February 1919

(Erase heading not required.)

Instructions regarding War Diaries and Intelligence Summaries are contained in F. S. Regs., Part II. and the Staff Manual respectively. Title pages will be prepared in manuscript.

Place	Date	Hour	Summary of Events and Information	Remarks and references to Appendices
MONT	Saturday 1st		Same billets. Usual duties. All mules attached to 3rd Cav Bde classified by Veterinary Board	JWS
"	Sunday 2nd		Same billets. Usual duties. Veterinary Board classified all mules attached to 6th Cav Bde	JWS
"	Monday 3rd		Same billets. Usual duties. Company H Qrs mules and horses classified by Remount Board	JWS
"	Tuesday 4th		Same billets. Usual duties. Sent one team to Animal Collecting Camp at ENGIS. Mules attached to 3rd Cav Bde classified by Remount Board	JWS
"	Wednesday 5th		Same billets. Usual duties. Sent another man for demobilization. Mules attached to 5th Cav Bde classified by Remount Board	JWS

Army Form C. 2118.

WAR DIARY
or
INTELLIGENCE SUMMARY
(Erase heading not required.)

2nd Cav Divnl.
Aux H T Coy RASC

Place	Date	Hour	Summary of Events and Information	Remarks and references to Appendices
MONT	Thursday 6th		Same trilers usual duties. Mules attached to 4 Cav Bde classified by veterinary and Remount Boards. Company H.Q. mules sent to THEUX for mallening	JHB
" "	Friday 7th		Same trelets Company H.Q. mules inspected by veterinary officer at THEUX	JHB
" "	Saturday 8th		Same trelets Sent 2 teams complete harns out to Cav. Corps 2 Store Depôt at SERAING	JHB
" "	Sunday 9th		Same trelets usual duties	JHB
" "	Monday 10th		Same trelets usual duties	JHB

Army Form C. 2118.

WAR DIARY
or
INTELLIGENCE SUMMARY

(Erase heading not required.)

February 1919 2nd Cav Div
Aux H Coy R.A.S.C.

Instructions regarding War Diaries and Intelligence Summaries are contained in F. S. Regs., Part II. and the Staff Manual respectively. Title pages will be prepared in manuscript.

Place	Date	Hour	Summary of Events and Information	Remarks and references to Appendices
MONT	Tuesday 11th		Same billets usual duties	AH3
	Wednesday 12th		Same billets usual duties	AH3
	Thursday 13th		Same billets usual duties	AH3
	Friday 14th		Same billets usual duties	AH3
	Saturday 15th		Same billets usual duties. S.S. M. Hitches and 2 NCOs sent to CONCENT for demobilization	AH3
	Sunday 16th		Same billets usual duties 3 more men sent for demobilization to CONCENT	AH3
	Monday 17th		Same billets usual duties	AH3
	Tuesday 18th		Same billets usual duties	AH3

Army Form C. 2118.

WAR DIARY
or
INTELLIGENCE SUMMARY.
(Erase heading not required.)

2nd Cav Divnl
Aux H T Coy R.A.S.C

February

Place	Date	Hour	Summary of Events and Information	Remarks and references to Appendices
MOINT	Wednesday 19th		Same betels usual duties. Two teams from each Brigade sent in today.	JHB
"	Thursday 20th		Same betels usual duties.	JHB
"	Friday 21st		Same betels usual duties. Arranged stabling for 80 animals at JEVOUMONT.	JHB
"	Saturday 22nd		Same betels usual duties. All teams from Brigades sent in today. N° 1 & 4 sections billeted at JEVOUMONT	JHB
"	Sunday 23rd		Same betels usual duties and inspections	JHB
"	Monday 24th		Same betels usual duties. Exchanged 92 Z mules for 93 X mules from 2nd Cav Reserve Park	JHB
"	Tuesday 25th		Same betels usual duties. Inspection of all animals by ADVS. Sent 2 Z horses to animal collecting camp at SERAING	JHB

Army Form C. 2118.

WAR DIARY
or
INTELLIGENCE SUMMARY.

February 1919   2nd Cav Div Aux HT Coy
                         R A S C

(Erase heading not required.)

Place	Date	Hour	Summary of Events and Information	Remarks and references to Appendices
MONT	Wednesday 26th		Same billets. Usual duties. Mules received from 2nd Cav Reserve Park very wild and the shortage of men causing some considerable anxiety	/HS
"	Thursday 27th		Same billets. Usual duties. Sent 13 mules marked D to 7th M.V.S. Sent 9 men to CONCENT for demobilization	/HS
"	Friday 28th		Same billets. Usual duties. Repairing wagons etc	/HS

A Brebner 2nd Lieut
O.C. 2nd Cav Div Aux HT Coy RASC

Confidential

WD 33

War Diary

of

2nd Cavalry Divisional Auxiliary Horse Transport Company

From 1st March 1919 to 31st March 1919.

(Volume LV).

Army Form C. 2118.

2nd Cav. Divn
Aux HT Coy R A S C

WAR DIARY
~~INTELLIGENCE SUMMARY.~~

(Erase heading not required.)

MARCH 1919

Instructions regarding War Diaries and Intelligence Summaries are contained in F. S. Regs., Part II. and the Staff Manual respectively. Title pages will be prepared in manuscript.

Place	Date	Hour	Summary of Events and Information	Remarks and references to Appendices
MONT	Saturday 1st		Same billets. Usual duties repairing wagons etc	JMB
"	Sunday 2nd		Same billets. Usual duties repairing wagons etc	JMB
"	Monday 3rd		Same billets. Usual duties. Handed over 63" 7 mules to OC 3rd Machine Gun Squadron. Also 11 men temporarily transferred	JMB
"	Tuesday 4th		Same billets. Usual duties. Sent returnable men to 1st Cav Div. Evacuated a mule to No. 7 MV Section	JMB
"	Wednesday 5th		Same billets. Usual duties. Sent 4 men to CONCENT for demobilization. Sent billeting party to GOFFONTAINE	JMB
"	Thursday 6th		Company moved to GOFFONTAINE at 0930 hours	JMB
GOFFONTAINE	Friday 7th		All animals under cover in factory. Water wagon attached HQ RASC sent back to Company	JMB
"	Saturday 8th		Same billets	JMB
"	Sunday 9th		Same billets. Sent 1 NCO and 9 men to guard Supply dump at PATTERN, GERMANY	JMB

Army Form C. 2118.

MARCH 1919 WAR DIARY or INTELLIGENCE SUMMARY.

2nd Cav Div Aux HT Coy Base

(Erase heading not required.)

Place	Date	Hour	Summary of Events and Information	Remarks and references to Appendices
OFFONTAINE	Monday 10th		Same billets, usual duties. Repairing wagons &c. Received 9 men from 2. 4. 5. C.T.O. to replace those sent to PATTERN	JAB
" "	Tuesday 11th		Same billets usual duties etc	JAB
" "	Wednesday 12th		Same billets usual duties. 3 repairable men sent to 5th M.G. Squadron	JAB
" "	Thursday 13th		Same billets usual duties. Received 100 Z mules from 1st Cav Division in exchange for 1 × horse and 99 × mules.	JAB
" "	Friday 14th		Same billets. Detailed 12 wagons and teams to report to O.C. 7th D.G.'s to convey stores to PEPINSTER	JAB
" "	Saturday 15th		Same billets. Same teams to PEPINSTER also 16 teams 3rd D.G's to draw unit vehicles to Railhead	JAB

Army Form C. 2118.

WAR DIARY
or
INTELLIGENCE SUMMARY

2nd New Div Aux HT Coy
R.A.S.C.

(Erase heading not required.)

Instructions regarding War Diaries and Intelligence Summaries are contained in F. S. Regs., Part II. and the Staff Manual respectively. Title pages will be prepared in manuscript.

MARCH

Place	Date	Hour	Summary of Events and Information	Remarks and references to Appendices
OFFONTAINE	Sunday 16		Same billets. Usual duties. Strength of Coy now raised to 80 men and 100 mules and 6 horses.	JMB
"	Monday 17		Same billets. Detailed 7 teams to report to D Battery, 7 teams and 15 pairs to J Battery, and 2 teams and 1 pair pairs to Hqrs RHA to draw Guns, Limbers etc to Railhead	JMB
"	Tuesday 18		Same billets. Sent gentry men for dismounted gun for men duties. Returned 20 pair wheelers & pair leaders 1 pair 4 Cav Bde at MERI. Cart to report H Qrs 4th Cav Bde at MERI	JMB
"	Wednesday 19		Same billets. Usual duties. 2/1 pairs sent to Hqr 4th Cav Bde yesterday brought in vehicles to PEPINSTER JMB Sent 6 x horses to 3rd Hussars	JMB
"	Thursday 20		Same billets. Usual duties etc overhauling leatherwork and wagons	JMB

MARCH 1919 WAR DIARY or INTELLIGENCE SUMMARY.

Army Form C. 2118.

2nd Cav Div A.H.T Coy R.A.S.C

Place	Date	Hour	Summary of Events and Information	Remarks and references to Appendices
OFFOINTAINE	Friday 21st		Same trekks Usual duties and inspections	AA13
" "	Saturday 22nd		Same trekks usual duties and inspections	AA3
" "	Sunday 23rd		Same trekks usual duties etc	AA3
" "	Monday 24th		Same trekks usual duties etc	AA3
" "	Tuesday 25th		Same trekks etc	AA3
" "	Wednesday 26th		Same trekks etc	AA3
" "	Thursday 27th		Same trekks Sent 17 teams Totters 8" Hussars at LAMBREMONT to draw units vehicles to PEPINSTER	AA3
" "	Friday 28th		Same trekks usual duties etc Received 2 Z horses from 4th DG's	AA3 AA3

Army Form C. 2118.

WAR DIARY
or
INTELLIGENCE SUMMARY. 2nd Can Div A.T. Coy R.A.S.C

(Erase heading not required.)

Place	Date	Hour	Summary of Events and Information	Remarks and references to Appendices
OFFONTAINE	Saturday 29th		Same below. Usual routine. 1 N.C.O and 6 men returned from Supply Dump at PATTERN	AWB
	Sunday 30th		Same billets. Usual routine. Sent 1 Warrant Officer 1 N.C.O and 7 men for Reorganization to CONCENT newly encaged to "N" Mobile Vet Section	AWB
	Monday 31st		Same billets. Usual duties etc. Strength of Company 1 Officer 76 O.R 99 mules 2 horses	AWB

J. M. Bretone Lieut
O.C. 2nd Can Div Aux H T Coy
R.A.S.C.

Confidential

Vol 34

War Diary

of

2nd Cavalry Divisional Auxiliary Horse Transport Company

From 1st April 1919 To 30th April 1919.

Volume (LVII).

Army Form C. 2118.

WAR DIARY
or
INTELLIGENCE SUMMARY.

2nd Cav Divl
Aux HT Coy RA.S.C.

(Erase heading not required.)

Place	Date	Hour	Summary of Events and Information	Remarks and references to Appendices
GOFFONTAINE	Sunday 1st		Same tricks. Usual routine overhauling equipment etc	MB
"	Wednesday 2nd		Same tricks. Usual duties. Evacuated 1 mule to No 7 Mobile Vet Section. 1 mule died from pneumonia	MB
"	Thursday 3rd		Same tricks. Usual duties. Received instructions from Staff Captain Cadre Brigade to the effect that the Company will be reduced to Cadre 'A'	MB
"	Friday 4th		Same tricks. Usual duties and inspection. OC RASC inspected Company Animal account.	MB
"	Saturday 5th		Same tricks. Usual duties. Services worn shoes etc	MB
"	Sunday 6th		Same tricks. Usual duties. Cleaning up generally. Marched over 80 mules with couple etc & harness to OC 3rd Cav Div Aux HT Coy	MB

Army Form C. 2118.

WAR DIARY
or
INTELLIGENCE SUMMARY.

April 1919 2nd Cav Divnl Aux H T Coy R A S C

(Erase heading not required.)

Place	Date	Hour	Summary of Events and Information	Remarks and references to Appendices
GOFFONTAINE	Monday 7th		Same billets usual duties	JMS
"	Tuesday 8th		Same billets usual duties Inspection of equipment etc	JMS
"	Wednesday 9th		Same billets usual duties Cleaning wagons etc Evacuated 1 mule blind 2 lame to No 7 Mobile Vet Section	JMS
"	Thursday 10th		Same billets usual duties cleaning wagons etc	JMS
"	Friday 11th		Same billets usual duties Inspection of mens equipment	JMS
			3 men reported from 7th Mobile Vet Section	
"	Saturday 12th		Same billets usual duties Inspection of equipment	JMS
"	Sunday 13th		Same billets usual duties Strength of Company 2 Offrs 83 ORs 16 mules 2 horses Captain R Embleton from 50th Divisional Train arrived to take over company.	JMS

Army Form C. 2118.

WAR DIARY
or
INTELLIGENCE SUMMARY.

APRIL 1919   2nd Cav Divnl Aux H.T. Coy
               R.A.S.C

Instructions regarding War Diaries and Intelligence Summaries are contained in F. S. Regs., Part II. and the Staff Manual respectively. Title pages will be prepared in manuscript.

(Erase heading not required.)

Place	Date	Hour	Summary of Events and Information	Remarks and references to Appendices
TOFFONTAINE	Monday 14th		Same billets usual duties. Sent 10 NCOs & men to CONCENT for demobilization	JMS
"	Tuesday 15th		Same billets usual duties moved company in to PEPINSTER	JMS
"	Wednesday 16th		Same billets usual duties	JMS
PEPINSTER	Thursday 17th		Same billets usual duties	JMS
"	Friday 18th		Same billets Inspection of Equipment etc by DADOS 2 Cav Div	JMS
"	Saturday 19th		Same billets Returned 12 G S wagons to Ordnance	JMS
"	Sunday 20th		Same billets usual duties etc	JMS
"	Monday 21st		Same billets usual duties etc	JMS
"	Tuesday 22nd		Same billets usual duties etc	JMS

APRIL 1919 WAR DIARY or INTELLIGENCE SUMMARY

Army Form C. 2118.

2nd Cav Divnl Aux H T Coy RASC

Place	Date	Hour	Summary of Events and Information	Remarks and references to Appendices
PEPINSTER	Wednesday 23rd		Same billets Detailed 9 pairs to move 3rd M.G Squadron vehicles to PEPINSTER Station from ENSIVAL	JWB
"	Thursday 24th		Same billets usual duties	JWB
"	Friday 25th		Same billets Detailed 9 pairs to move 4th M.G Squadron vehicles to PEPINSTER Station from VERVIERS Sent 15 men to 8th Auxiliary Horse Company	JWB
"	Saturday 26th		Same billets Detailed 9 pairs to move 5th M.G Squadron vehicles to PEPINSTER Station from JUSLENVILLE	JWB
"	Sunday 27th		Same billets usual duties etc	JWB
"	Monday 28th		Same billets	JWB
"	Tuesday 29th		Same billets	JWB
"	Wednesday 30th		Same billets	JWB

JWBrebner Lieut for Capt-
OC 2nd Cav Div Aux H T Coy RASC

WAR DIARY
INTELLIGENCE SUMMARY

Army Form C. 2118.

2nd Gas Bn
A.H.T.G

Place	Date	Hour	Summary of Events and Information	Remarks and references to Appendices
PEPINSTER (BELGIUM)	May 1919 12th to 21st		During 12th to 21st the unit we have received the same difficulties but more or less the same bad status — during a little transition period — hungry much, lack of bath water, (the Quarters of PRINTER where we were are not Z's & L.D. then were large barracks — the moment for the night into the country — every man was taken to England up & Discharged — Officers into the country — we without Coats — a Board covering Sick went with Men — but that in means had been taken to try Rationing Scheme, that bathrooms equally refused has been given — even to account we are short though not in Stock. During period 41 OR + Other have been reported dead. 2 hospital — all the arrival have been transferred to the No 4 Base Spares JAMBES. Every effort being made to retain at strength. Sport has introduced + showing discredit moving to delay the return away. Every man it can be carrying — many are to draw of new + comfort forwarded to them.	

John Cuddie

WAR DIARY
or
INTELLIGENCE SUMMARY.
(Erase heading not required.)

Army Form C. 2118.

June 1919

Place	Date	Hour	Summary of Events and Information	Remarks and references to Appendices
Billets, PEPINSTER.	1/6/19	—	Total Strength 22 all ranks, 1 OR on leave. While Estre acting as Equipment Guard — no other duties. Sent in A.I. 1531. — Showing N.L. cars balance at end of May a/c. Enjoyed RASC/631 between — duties. cleaning truck.	
"	2/6/19	"	Same duties as above. Received instructions from O' Sql Lines t.s.c. to get R Enlistees to proceed to 2Bn G RAFC for duty — unless Sub Une wishes further utilisation of Handing in cars etc. — has refused to comply with I.C. R AFC 2nd Bn Tin — Proceeding to HUSSEY fountain — was instructed to await further return.	
	3/6/19	"	Same Billets. Same duties generally. — Received return from Estre Pets H.Q. to proceed with Friend until next visit to proceed until further return. There have been —	
	4.5/6/19	"	Same billets. Same duties as above. 3 ORs departed to Trunk leaving strength now 19 men + 16 - OR (10R on leave Returned with D) Back to I.C. RASC experiment order to remain with them until further instruction have been received.	
	6.6.19	"	Same Billet. — all Strength now doing duty as Equipment Guard + cleaning the 40 double Cab of Lorries which Via European Gun 3 ton Aux (Truck) in a very dirty condition.	
	7.6.19	"	Same Billets. Same duties.	

Army Form C. 2118.

WAR DIARY
INTELLIGENCE SUMMARY.
(Erase heading not required.)

Instructions regarding War Diaries and Intelligence Summaries are contained in F. S. Regs., Part II. and the Staff Manual respectively. Title pages will be prepared in manuscript.

June 1919

Place	Date	Hour	Summary of Events and Information	Remarks and references to Appendices
B.Wk PEPINSTER	8/6/19		Some autos & Equipment Served. Identity noted. 1st officer entered off. with Common Paymaster Pepn.	631 ASC
	9/6/19		Ordinary routine of Guard, cleaning & fatigue	
	10/6/19		" " " "	
	11/6/19		" " " "	
	12/6/19		" " " "	
	13/6/19		" " " "	
	14/6/19		" " " " autos returned in Coy of Coy Ho. ASC	
	15/6/19		" " " "	
	16/6/19		" " " " Guard. cleaning fatigues	
	17/6/19		" " " "	
	18/6/19		" " " "	
	19/6/19		Packed wagons ready for entrainment. Coy handed over to 281 Coy R.E. Lt. Col. W. Evans Elliott D.S.O.	
	20/6/19		entraining aspect of 281 Coy R.E. Lt. Col. (?)	
	21/6/19		Entries Officer N.C.I. Entrainment 5775 Coy R.A.S.C. were entrained and proceeded to	
	22/6/19		ANTWERP, for shipment to England at 10 am. J — them proceeded to	
	23.6.19		report to 281 Coy R.A.S.C. HARVE.	

R.J. Sutcliffe Capt.
O.C. 2nd Coy S.S. A.H.T. Coy.

www.ingramcontent.com/pod-product-compliance
Lightning Source LLC
Chambersburg PA
CBHW080912230426
43667CB00015B/2656